FAT! SO?

FAT! SO?

Because you **DON'T** have to
apologize for your size!

Marilyn Wann

TEN SPEED PRESS
Berkeley

All rights reserved. Published in the United States by Ten Speed Press, an imprint of
the Crown Publishing Group, a division of Random House, Inc., New York.
www.crownpublishing.com
www.tenspeed.com

Ten Speed Press and the Ten Speed Press colophon are registered trademarks of
Random House, Inc.

Excerpt on page 21 from Brain Droppings by George Carlin. ©1997, Comedy Concepts, Inc.
Reprinted with permission by Hyperion.

Library of Congress Cataloging-in Publication Data

Wann, Marilyn.
        Fat!So?: Because you don't have to apologize for your size!/
    Marilyn Wann.
            p. cm.
    Includes index.
    1. Body image. 2. Overweight women—Psychology. 3.Obesity—
Psychological aspects. 4. Feminine beauty (Aesthetics) 5. Self-esteem in women. I. Title.
BF697.5.B63W25   1999
306.4—dc21   98-27145
                                                                         CIP

ISBN-13: 978-0-89815-995-0 (alk. paper)

Printed in Canada

Cover and interior design by Paul Kepple
Cover art by Ron Sol

15 14 13 12 11 10 9 8 7 6 5

First Edition

CONTENTS

FIRM SUPPORT

This book could not have been written without firm support from tons of fabulous people. Heartfelt thanks go to my ever-loving parents, Ella Lou and Harold Wann, for making *FAT!SO?* possible, and to every single subscriber, for making *FAT!SO?* real. I am also forever grateful to my wonderful colleagues Cath Thompson and Heather Urban, for all their work and dedication, without which I'd still be trying to get to the printer with issue number three; Debora Iyall, for her art; Sondra Solovay, for her brilliant research; Geoffrey Dryvynsyde, for Thursday; Haley Hertz, for being first reader; Regina Bauer, for everything from chicken wrangling to kitchen detail; Copy Central/Castro and One World Café, for their indulgence; Chris Hanson and Ron Avitzur, for their enthusiasm and spare computer parts; Lynn McAfee, for blazing the trail; Daniel Pinkwater, for the wisdom; and James Baldwin, for the inspiration. I relied on the collections and the kind reference librarians at the San Francisco Public Library, Main Branch, and the University of California at San Francisco Medical School Library. And of course, I am grateful to the National Association to Advance Fat Acceptance, for providing a forum in which I could explore the meaning of flabulousness.

INTRODUCTION

ON OCTOBER 26, 1993, I HAD A REALLY BAD day. First, the guy I was dating said he was embarrassed to introduce me to friends because I was fat (ouch!). Then, Blue Cross of California decided not to give me health insurance because of my weight (double ouch!). I was stunned, hurt, outraged.

Now if you've ever been stunned *and* hurt *and* outraged, you know how hard it is to feel all of these things at once. Pretty soon, you have to pick one feeling. Stunned and hurt are great emotions, but they really aren't very useful. So I chose outrage.

All my life, I had done everything I could to make sure people accepted me, maybe even liked me, *despite* my fat. I was a good student, a trustworthy friend, an obedient child. I didn't speak unless I was sure I had something interesting or amusing to say. I went out of my way to be considerate, supportive, a good listener. But if no one wanted to hang out, I was quite content with my own company. As a fat teenager, I never expected to wear trendy clothes or get invited to the prom. I had friends, but never

felt like part of the crowd. Instead, I focused on the areas where I knew I could succeed.

All of the independence and communication skills that I developed as a fat child started to pay off in unexpected ways. I loved to write, so I became editor of my high school newspaper. I was good at school, so I earned two degrees from Stanford. I wasn't afraid of being alone, so I traveled all over Europe and Russia by myself, having adventures.

In fact, I wasn't really afraid of much, since I figured the worst had already happened to me—I was fat.

In that fearless mode, I learned how to fly an airplane. In college, I threw brilliant parties and developed a wonderful circle of friends. Over the years, I learned to trust that my personality and charm could attract men. But some part of me always discounted that attention. Some part of me was afraid that if I stopped trying, I wouldn't count for anything. After all, I was fat.

Then, on October 26, 1993, my worst fears came true. None of it mattered: the accomplishments, the personality, all the extra effort.

9

Being fat outweighed everything else about me. I am five-feet four-inches tall, and I weigh 270 pounds. My blood pressure, cholesterol, and blood sugars—the three best health indicators —are all normal. I have no history of serious illness. I don't smoke. I exercise and eat my vegetables. I brush my teeth and pay my taxes and wear a seat belt, yet from my most personal moments (with that guy) to my official business

speak up about the kind of mistreatment I experienced on that really bad day. Staying silent would mean that I agreed to being mistreated, to being banished from life and from love—and I most certainly do not agree to that!

* * *

The day after that really bad day, I started a zine—my way of speaking up. I should explain that a zine (short for *magazine*) is a kind of low-

QUESTION: If you got together all of the
AMERICANS WHO ARE ON DIETS RIGHT NOW,
how many states would they populate?
ANSWER: TWENTY-SEVEN

(with that insurance company), I was shut out because of a number on a scale.

So I sat there on that really bad day, deciding between stunned and hurt and outraged. I thought about what my date had said. I thought about what Blue Cross had said. And I realized that I absolutely did not agree with them. Fat was not a death sentence; it was just a fact. I decided that if a guy couldn't accept my weight, he didn't get to date me. I decided that Blue Cross's label of "morbid obesity" wasn't a diagnosis; it was discrimination. I decided I had to

budget, alternative publication. People start zines for the same reason Thomas Paine was inspired to write his revolutionary pamphlet *Common Sense*—they have an urgent desire to take a stand on the major issue of the day.

Thanks to my journalism background, publishing a zine was the kind of work I already knew, but I needed a name for my zine. I thought about all of the names kids called me in third grade: One-Ton, Henrietta Hippo, or just plain Fatso. Then I thought about other groups of people who no longer allow themselves to be put

CASUALLY MENTION FAT AS A CONVERSATIONAL TOPIC, WITHOUT TALKING ABOUT LOSING WEIGHT.

down for who they are. For example, lesbians and gay men who defiantly answer to *queer*. I thought about how I'd always avoided the word *fat*. Now I wanted to come out as a proud fat person. I wanted to show that the names really couldn't hurt me anymore. I thought again about being called Fatso as a child, how painful and damning that word felt then. But I *was* fat, I *am* fat! So? I didn't look up to see whether a lightbulb actually went on over my head, but that's what it felt like. I knew at that moment I simply had to publish *FAT!SO?*—the zine for people who don't apologize for their size.

Well, after six months of the hardest work I've ever done, I printed 1,000 copies of the first *FAT!SO?*, sure that I'd never get rid of them all, but they sold out. I printed 1,000 more and sold all of them, too.

I had offered a subscription rate almost as a joke. Then checks started filling the P.O. box I'd rented at the last minute (yikes!). Here were hundreds of people I didn't even know, wanting to buy my zine. I would have to do *FAT!SO?* again (double yikes!). But the letters from those new subscribers made me believe that I *could* keep doing the zine—that there was plenty to say about what it's like to be fat. People wrote about how they'd longed all their lives to read

something like *FAT!SO?*, how I'd made them laugh, how they felt good about themselves for the first time. Opening the post office box was like waking up on Christmas morning, and each letter in that box made me more and more determined to continue.

At that point, I knew it was time to come out to my parents about *FAT!SO?*. I'd kept it a secret until I had something I could show them. I flew home with a stack of hot-pink zines in my carry-on, incredibly nervous. I rehearsed what I'd say: "Excuse me Mom and Dad, but, in case you hadn't noticed, I'm fat." The minute we got in from the airport, I handed them copies, with the warning that they might not like it. That first issue of *FAT!SO?* had stories from people of all sizes. It had Roseanne sightings and a quiz and an advice column. It also had something I called "Anatomy Lesson": a series of photos of variously shaped butts. I wanted people to see that not everyone looks like Kate Moss. It was visual counterpropaganda. I was certain my parents would disown me. After all, I had published a photo of my naked butt and distributed it nationwide. Well, they thought it was hilarious. My mother, who has been fat all her life, had tears in her eyes. My dad gave me business advice. I couldn't have asked for a better, more

CORRECT PEOPLE WHEN THEY USE EUPHEMISMS FOR SIZE. SAY, "I PREFER THE WORD FAT. IT'S MORE POLITE."

supportive response. That was nearly five years ago. Since then, *FAT!SO?* has shown up on *Oprah* and on MTV. It was written up in *USA Today*, the *Washington Post*, and *Glamour*. *Utne Reader* nominated *FAT!SO?* for its Alternative Press Award in both 1995 and 1996, the first two years of the zine's existence.

Through it all, *FAT!SO?* has made it possible for me to do things I never thought I could do.

ically now that I don't apologize for my size. And I did finally succeed in getting health insurance (I just have to pay four times more than a thin person does). Best of all, thanks to *FAT!SO?*, I've met wonderful people of all sizes. I've learned that you can absolutely be happy and healthy and successful—and fat. In fact, you can be out-and-out fabulous at any size. I wrote this book to share the *FAT!SO?* attitude with as many people

IN SWEDISH, SVELTE MEANS "TO STARVE."

I've gone on TV and radio, been quoted in newspapers. I've shamelessly announced what I weigh to thousands of people. I've jumped at the chance to take on Richard Simmons and former surgeon general C. Everett Koop—two men who just love to make fat people feel bad. I've dyed my hair hot pink to match the zine, led flirting workshops for fat people, and modeled a thong bikini to show off my, um, fat pride. I've given presentations to high school and college students, explaining how people are *supposed* to come in all sizes, so it's not okay to mistreat the fat ones (*or* the thin ones, for that matter).

The final outcome of that really bad day? Let's just say that my love life has improved dramat-

as possible, because life is too short for self-hatred and celery sticks, because you don't deserve even one really bad day, because you don't have to apologize for your size.

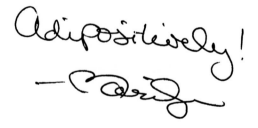

Adipositively!
—Marilyn

WHAT
ARE YOU SO
AFRAID OF?

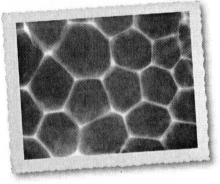

THIS IS WHAT A FAT CELL LOOKS LIKE—A healthy, normal, human fat cell.

Jobs are lost, lovers forsaken, lives postponed—all because of fat cells like this one. A $40 billion industry thrives on the hatred of these graceful, lipid spheres. Millions of people fight a war of starvation against them every day. Most Americans would rather get hit by a truck than get fat. Amputation of a leg is preferable. Some would rather die.

Fear of fat does nothing for you except get in your way. I know from experience. Being afraid of fat won't impress a date or advance your career or make your family closer. It doesn't whiten teeth or balance your bank account or cure depression. I guarantee that worrying about your weight won't make you look better in your clothes, or out of them. Fear of fat is like a cloud over your head. It's not attractive. Ask yourself, what has body anxiety done for me lately? Nothing good, right? So why not get rid of it???

Now, since you're holding this book and reading this page, you've already started to conquer that fear. Woohoooooooo! Good for you!

Perhaps I sound crazy. But I know lots of people who've conquered their fear of fat. You *can* face your fears. You *can* dispel that cloud. And you don't have to change the world to do it. You don't even have to change your weight. You just have to change your attitude. It'd be my honor to act as your friendly tour guide on the trip from the old attitude (fear of fat) to the new attitude: *flabulousness!*

First stop on the tour: Take another look at the photo. This is the actual, physical stuff you're talking about when you say that you hate your fat. Is this fat photo scary? Ugly? Evil? Nope. Compared to some of the things you might see

COMPLIMENT YOUR FAT FRIENDS ON THEIR APPEARANCE. DO IT SINCERELY AND WITH NO "BUTS."

on a real-life surgery TV show, this fat photo is not at all gruesome. In fact, it is simple, elegant, even beautiful. Its clean lines, gentle curves, and bold patterns have the kind of innate style that fashion designers aspire to. Nothing about this fat cell should inspire fear and loathing on a national level.

It's actually quite rare to find a photograph of a human fat cell. In fact, this photo was the only one I could locate anywhere in the entire country. I got it from a retired Harvard Medical School professor who lives in Missoula, Montana. He explained that scientists don't study fat cells very much because nothing much goes wrong with them. It's true.

A hundred years ago, Woods Hutchinson (the C. Everett Koop of his day) called fat cells "one of the most peaceable, useful, and law-abiding of all our tissues" and "a most harmless, healthful, innocent tissue." (Laura Fraser, author of *Losing It: False Hopes and Fat Profits in the Diet Industry*, found these quotes in *Cosmopolitan* and *Saturday Evening Post*.)

The same thing is true today, as I discovered during a visit to the library of the University of California at San Francisco, a top-ranked medical school. The UCSF library is on a hill not far from where I live. It has great views of the Golden Gate Bridge and the ocean beyond, so doing research there isn't a hardship. While I was there, I checked the library catalog for books about fat cells, or adipocytes, as doctors call them. Guess how many books I found. One. Only one book! I challenge you to think of a single medical topic on which a world-renowned medical library would possess only one volume. In comparison, the UCSF library houses at least 2,859 books about cancer, not to mention all the journals and papers on the subject.

The average human body contains between twenty billion and forty billion fat cells. Even if our pals the adipocytes don't warrant much shelf space in the med-school stacks, they are important for your health. Fat cells keep you warm in winter, protect your internal organs from injury, and allow you to float blissfully in the swimming pool on a summer afternoon. Fat enables women to menstruate and protects against osteoporosis, one of the major killers of women. What's more, fat prevents wrinkles and gives you sexy curves. Without the awesome energy resources of your fat, you'd find it tough to skip breakfast or run a marathon or bear children. Fat is a necessary part of the human body, just like brain cells and blood cells, and just like them, fat represents life.

A IS FOR APPETITE

"Nothing in the world arouses more false hopes than the first four hours of a diet."
—anonymous

"I am going to have my dinner, After which I shan't be thinner."
—Jane Austen, *The Juvenilia of Jane Austen*

"Two or three things I know for sure, And one of them is that if we are
not beautiful to each other,
We cannot know beauty in any form."
—Dorothy Allison, author

QUIZ:
ARE YOU A FATSO?

YOU MAY THINK THAT ALL IT TAKES TO BE A fatso is a few extra pounds, some cellulite, maybe a jowl or two. Pinch an inch, and you're in the club. No, no, no, Chicamundi! If being a fatso were easy, what would become of the $40 billion diet industry? The fatso life takes attitude. It takes existential credentials (the kind that come from being an outcast and fighting self-hatred at the same time). It takes laughing at Jenny Craig commercials and voting for the fat Elvis and still, for some reason, lying about your weight on your driver's license. A fatso doesn't postpone life hoping to lose that extra 5 or 10 or 100 pounds. A real fatso does *not* apologize for size!

Find out if you've got what it takes to be a flabulous fatso. No cheating now.

1. **In grammar school, when we teamed up for kickball, I was**
   - ❐ **a.** Picked first.
   - ❐ **b.** Out sick with chicken pox.
   - ❐ **c.** Team captain.
   - ❐ **d.** Picked last and assigned to deep outfield.

2. **I drink diet Coke because**
   - ❐ **a.** It tastes so good.
   - ❐ **b.** I'm a big Paula Abdul fan.
   - ❐ **c.** People might look at me funny if I drink something with food value.
   - ❐ **d.** I want to commune with lab rats.

3. **I would pay four bucks for a headset on the airplane if they showed**
   - ❐ **a.** A *Buns of Steel* video.
   - ❐ **b.** Anything with Kim Basinger.
   - ❐ **c.** *The Nutty Professor.*
   - ❐ **d.** Old *Roseanne* episodes.

FILL YOUR HOME WITH FAT-POSITIVE ART. TOSS OUT THOSE WEIRD LITTLE LLADRÓ STATUES,
OR ANYTHING THAT PROMOTES STEREOTYPED BODY IMAGES.

4. If a clothing store has nothing that fits me, I
- ❒ **a.** Leave feeling worthless and depressed.
- ❒ **b.** Try on the one garment they have that barely fits me and buy it even if it's ugly.
- ❒ **c.** Tell the clerk that I prefer muumuus anyway.
- ❒ **d.** Come back with a flamethrower.

5. When we have sex, my lover
- ❒ **a.** Says I'm sexy, as long as I don't gain weight.
- ❒ **b.** Makes sure the lights are out.
- ❒ **c.** Makes hippopotamus jokes.
- ❒ **d.** Delights in my body just the way it is.

6. My ideal lover is
- ❒ **a.** Slim, physically fit, trim, petite, thin, skinny, athletic, height-weight proportional, and small-boned.
- ❒ **b.** A financially secure nonsmoker who enjoys sunset walks on the beach.
- ❒ **c.** Into mountain biking, hiking, roller-blading, and the occasional marathon.
- ❒ **d.** Built for comfort, not for speed.

7. When I see fat people, I want to
- ❒ **a.** Vomit.
- ❒ **b.** Suggest a diet, because I am so concerned for their health.
- ❒ **c.** Congratulate myself for being thin and therefore superior.
- ❒ **d.** Give them a smile because I know how brave they must be.

8. When I see waiflike supermodel Kate Moss, I want to
- ❒ **a.** Vomit three times a day so I can look just like her.
- ❒ **b.** Suggest a nutritional diet, because I am so concerned for her health.
- ❒ **c.** Congratulate her for doing such a lifelike impression of a stick figure.
- ❒ **d.** Give her a copy of *FAT!SO?* and a big fat hug.

9. When I go to the fridge for a snack, my mom/spouse/roommate says,
- ❒ **a.** "You aren't going to eat that, are you?"
- ❒ **b.** "You don't need that. Put it back."
- ❒ **c.** "Are you eating again?"
- ❒ **d.** "Bring me some, too, dear."

10. My favorite song lyrics are
- ❒ **a.** "She wore an itsy-bitsy, teeny-weeny, yellow polka-dot bikini."
- ❒ **b.** "And-a-one. Two. Three. Four. Now jog it out!"
- ❒ **c.** "Nobody's gettin' fat except Mama Cass."
- ❒ **d.** "R-E-S-P-E-C-T! Find out what it means to me!"

11. Me, fat? I would rather

☐ **a.** Die.

☐ **b.** Not think about it. It gives me the creeps.

☐ **c.** Spend thousands of dollars on diet products and hundreds of hours at the gym—and still live in fear of that extra five pounds.

☐ **d.** Accept it and get on with life.

12. I feel good about myself when

☐ **a.** My jeans fit.

☐ **b.** My weight is within height/weight chart recommendations.

☐ **c.** What a silly question! I'll never be skinny enough to feel okay.

☐ **d.** I can ignore society's messages about the ideal body and listen instead to my own truth.

13. My bumper sticker says,

☐ **a.** No fat chicks!

☐ **b.** Jazzercize!

☐ **c.** Honk if you love celery!

☐ **d.** Wide load.

14. I hate fat people because

☐ **a.** They smell.

☐ **b.** It makes me feel good about myself.

☐ **c.** It's hard for me to look at them; they just aren't normal.

☐ **d.** Not! There's no earthly reason to hate fat people.

15. I love fat people because

☐ **a.** They're so jolly.

☐ **b.** I feel skinny next to them.

☐ **c.** They're nurturing.

d. I understand and admire fat people.

Answers: D is the fabulous fatso response in each case.

B IS FOR BEAUTY

"Unnecessary dieting is because everything from television to fashion ads have made it seem wicked to cast a shadow. This wild, emaciated look appeals to some women, though not to many men, who are seldom seen pinning up a Vogue illustration in a machine shop."
—Peg Bracken, *The I Hate to Cook Book*

"Beware of sudden change in any great point of diet."
—Francis Bacon, *Of Regimen and Health*

"Hungry people cannot be good at learning or producing anything except, perhaps, violence."
—Pearl Bailey, *Pearl's Kitchen*

WHEN SOMEONE TELLS YOU IT LOOKS LIKE YOU'VE LOST WEIGHT, DO NOT TAKE IT AS A COMPLIMENT.

WHY I ENCOURAGE YOU TO USE THE F-WORD

THE MOST POWERFUL WORD IN THE ENGLISH language is the F-word. Not *that* one. Sadly, that F-word lost its zing circa 1983. Nonetheless, there's still an F-word around that packs a wallop, shatters a taboo or two, and makes strong men shudder—all before breakfast. That F-word, friends, is *fat*.

If you've been paying attention thus far, you've read the F-word approximately 97 times. Has it gotten any easier? A little bit? Good. I firmly believe the F-word is your friend.

It's a powerful friend, too. If you really want to bug folks, call them fat, especially if they're not. Then watch them howl in denial, burst into anger ("How could you be so mean?"), and finally worry themselves sick that they really are fat. Tell me one other word or phrase that can produce such strong reactions: "Root canal?"; "IRS audit?"; "License and registration, please?" None of these phrases have the elegant emotional impact of this one little word, *fat*, which is why the bullies use it against you, me, and anyone whom the bullies think can be made to feel smaller (or bigger) than they actually are.

That's why it's time to take this powerful, awe-inspiring word back from the bullies! It's time to put *fat* into the hands of people who will use its power for good, not evil! It's time, my fat brothers and sisters, for us to embrace the F-word!!!

When you claim the word *fat*, no one can use it against you ever again. Imagine that. Aunt Gladys tells you you're fat, and you say, "Yes, I am. Thanks for noticing!" Does she blink? Yes. Does she go up in a puff of smoke? No. Does she stop pestering you? Most likely.

Reclaiming the word *fat* is the miracle cure you've been looking for, the magic trick that makes all your worries about weight disappear. Do you want to feel good about yourself? Silence your tormentors? Look better in miniskirts? Use the F-word. Dorothy made her wish come true by saying, "There's no place like home." Well, I'm not Glenda the Good Witch, but I'm here to tell you that all you have to say is the magic word, *fat*. Say it loud, say it proud: Fat! Fat! Fat! Shake your belly three times and there you are, at home in your body, free from the guilt and the shame, the stress and the starvation, and the self-hatred. (And yes, when you use the F-word, you carry yourself with pride—so you will indeed look brilliant in above-the-knee fashions.) The trick is to really believe that there's no place like home, that there's nowhere you'd rather be than in the wonderful body you already have.

What's this? You can't even say the word? *Fat?* It's such a little word. It really won't hurt you to say it. I promise.

Some people can't pronounce the word *nuclear.* Others have problems saying *astigmatism, arthroscopy,* or *Worcestershire sauce.* But the F-word is straight out of Dick & Jane: *cat, bat, rat, sat, . . . fat.* See how easy?

Try sneaking up on it. First, say something easy. For example, *infatuated.* Try saying it to yourself whenever you're alone, perhaps when you're driving in your car (try not to hit anything). Doing this at ATMs is a great crime deterrent, too. Now, drop all those boring prefixes and suffixes from *infatuated* until you're left with one incredibly powerful syllable, *fat.*

Perhaps you resist the F-word because it doesn't seem like a polite thing to say. I would argue that it's actually the least offensive, sim-

plest word on the subject. Consider the unpleasant alternatives:

✳ **Overweight.** Over *whose* weight? Everyone has their own unique weight that's right for them. The right weight for some people means being fat, just like other people are naturally thin. Even doctors, nowadays, admit that those height/weight charts are bogus, so there really is no weight to be over. Aside from being judgmental and mean, the word *overweight* is just plain meaningless.

✳ **Obese.** This is a doctor's fancy way of saying, "I'm looking at you, and I find you disgusting. Would you like to buy this ineffective but wildly expensive weight-loss treatment? If you don't, you could die. Besides, my country club membership fees are due."

It's hard to diagnose "obesity." The number on the scale has very little to do with how healthy a person is. The diet specialists never seem to settle on a definition of *obese* (they just know it when they see it). Given the subjective nature of this term, you probably shouldn't put much weight on it as a diagnosis.

Another problem with the word *obese* is that health insurance companies love to use it as an excuse to deny fat people coverage, even when we're healthy. That's not a diagnosis either;

19

that's discrimination! Plus, a diagnosis of "obesity" can be used to justify barbaric treatments that doctors could never get away with inflicting on thin patients.

No lab-coat tone of voice can disguise the sneer contained in the word *obese*. It's the O-word. The *only* thing anyone can diagnose, just by looking at a fat person, is the viewer's own level of prejudice toward fat people.

❋ The euphemisms. *Heavy, large, voluptuous, zaftig, big-boned*—you only need a euphemism if you find the truth distasteful. But there is nothing wrong with being fat, so there's nothing wrong with using the word. It's just as polite to say *fat* as it is to say *young* or *tall* or *human*.

I remember the moment when my flying instructor told me I was ready to solo. I couldn't believe it was happening. I was all alone in the plane. I took off (that's the easy part). Then I realized that I was 1,000 feet up in the air, and the only person who could get me back down was me. Luckily, I was practiced and ready. My landing went just fine. You're ready for your solo flight with the F-word, now, too. The preceding pages have gotten you warmed up and ready. I'll leave you alone for a minute. Close the book, find someone to practice with, and say it. It might just be fun.

SPEAK UP FOR YOURSELF. DON'T LET FAT-HATING REMARKS SLIDE.

C IS FOR CORRECT

"You probably noticed, elsewhere I use the word fat. I used that word because that's what fat people are. They're fat. They're not large; they're not stout, chunky, hefty, or plump. And they're not big-boned. Dinosaurs are big-boned. These people are not necessarily obese, either. Obese is a medical term. (Author's note: A particularly meaningless term, at that.) And they're not overweight. Overweight implies there is some correct weight.

There is no correct weight. Heavy is also a misleading term. An aircraft carrier is heavy; it's not fat. Only people are fat, and that's what fat people are. They're fat. I offer no apology for this. It is not intended as criticism or insult. It is simply descriptive language. I don't like euphemisms. Euphemisms are a form of lying. Fat people are not gravitationally disadvantaged. They're fat. I prefer seeing things the way they are, not the way some people wish they were."

—George Carlin, *Brain Droppings*

SPEAK UP FOR OTHER FAT PEOPLE WHENEVER YOU CAN. SHOW THEM HOW IT'S DONE.

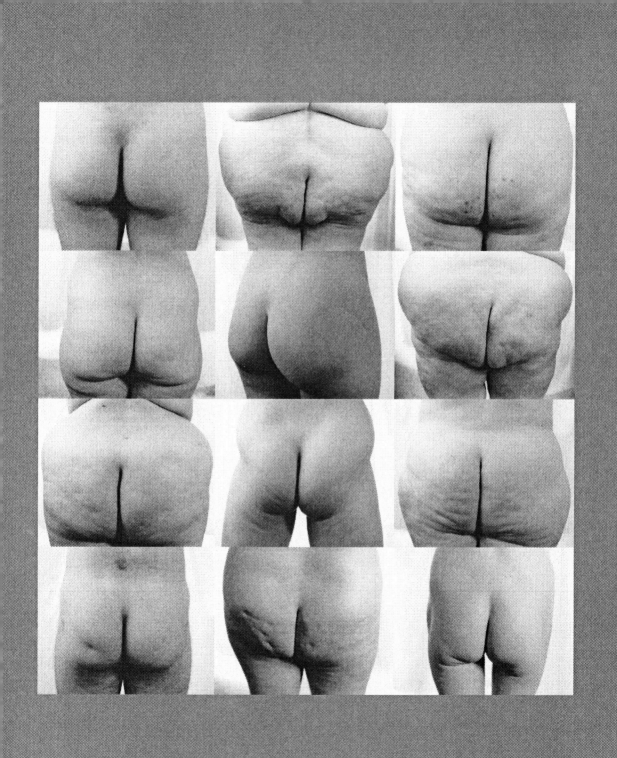

ANATOMY LESSON #1

THE BUTT

WHAT DO YOU LIKE ABOUT BEING FAT?

F YOU'RE LIKE MOST PEOPLE, YOU'VE SPENT plenty of time worrying about your weight. In all that time, it probably never occurred to you to ask yourself what you actually *like* about being fat. Who would ask such a thing? Just formulating the question goes against all our conditioning (and is probably illegal in the state of Mississippi). Nonetheless, the question that no one thinks to ask always produces the most interesting answer. (Einstein said that. Or maybe it was Barbara Walters.)

That's why the survey on the *FAT!SO?* Web site asks people, "What do you like about being fat?" So far, hundreds of people have generated thousands of interesting answers to this question. Laid end to end, their responses are powerful counterpropaganda to the forces that would have you believe you have to be thin to be happy. I'll list some of the best answers here. You can try them on for size or think up your own.

* My friends like me for who I am.
* I'm unique, not a cookie-cutter person.
* Looking younger than my age—no wrinkles.
* People like to hug a soft person.
* Looking like a fertility goddess.
* People get out of my way when I'm in a hurry.
* I've never been mugged.
* I can eat what I like (including salads).
* People remember me.
* Having big, luscious breasts.
* Not being on a diet.
* I exercise because I want to, not because I have to.
* When I was in the Middle East, a young woman said, "You're so fat! How did you do it?"
* I can do something fun, instead of obsessing about my thighs.
* I am part of the fat modeling scene.
* My girlfriend is fat. I wouldn't trade her for the world.
* My measurements won't be all I have going for me.
* I'm not tiny and helpless.
* I feel substantial.
* It makes me strong.
* It taught me to think for myself and not rely on the crowd.
* It made me more accepting of other people

WEAR SOMETHING THAT REVEALS A BODY PART YOU DON'T NORMALLY SHOW OFF.

who are different.

* It's a built-in jerk detector.
* I have weight behind my efforts.
* I have more body to tattoo.
* It gives me attitude.
* I just plain feel good the way I am.
* It's part of me, and I like myself.

And the answers from one thirteen-year-old guy:

* A keg is more than a six-pack.
* If you've got the size, you win the prize.

What do *you* like about being fat?

1. _____

2. _____

3. _____

LOVE IN THE TIME OF SIZE 18

by Alexis Neptune

ONCE HAD A BOYFRIEND WHO SAID THAT WHEN he held my butt, he felt like he was holding four. I should have told him that he was damn lucky to hold it at all, but that weak girl I once was cried and didn't eat for three days. I once had a boyfriend who bought me a dress in a size

6. When I asked him why he bought it in that size, he said, "As incentive." I cried and went on Nutri-System. I was a size 6 for a full eleven months and then had my gallbladder removed at age twenty-one.

I've gone from a size 6 to a size 18 and back, again and again. I've been on every diet you can think of. I have done aerobics, callanetics, weight lifting, jogging, you name it. My body still cries out, "I am 180 pounds and a size 16, and nothing you can do will change that!" I have come to accept it, begrudgingly at first. Now there are things that I like about my flesh. For instance, my motherly breasts, the huge arch from my waist to my knee, my grandma's legs—like an heirloom. I still have bad days. They come mostly when I need new clothes, but they are growing farther apart.

I had a boyfriend who oohed and melted with just a look from me. When I cried that I was fat, he said, "You're my beauty queen." He took me to meet his mother. She was round like an apple and soft, freckled with these blue, kind eyes. She asked me why I was so skinny. She fed me fresh tomato sandwiches from her garden. I told the boy I loved his mom. He said that she was the second most beautiful girl in the world—that I was the first. I married him.

LITTLE LOST POUND O' FAT SEES THE WORLD

WAS FLIPPING THROUGH A MAIL-ORDER CATalog one day, when I came across something mesmerizing—a blob of fake fat. I knew I had to have one, but I didn't know why. They wanted $24.95 for a pound of slimy, jiggly plastic, its curdlike surface embossed with the words "1 LB. FAT." That's $24.95 *plus* shipping and handling, and it isn't even the real thing!

Just think. Let's say I weigh 270 pounds and I'm about 50 percent fat. What am I worth? A cool $3,368.25 at the very *least*. Of course, I'd never be willing to sell, but I find it quite amusing to think of people who are so desperate for a few extra pounds that they'll lay down twenty-five bucks for a shoddy look-alike, an expensive substitute.

I know that's not what the fake fat manufacturers had in mind—their customers are mainly those crazy diet-group leaders who use blobs of fake fat as a motivational tool—but I couldn't imagine that anyone would actually *believe* they have jiggly, plastic blobs inside their bodies.

Then it hit me. The pound of ersatz fat doesn't represent the pound you *weigh,* it's the pound you *lose,* which poses a deep, metaphysical question: Where *does* a pound of fat go when you lose it? (It has to go somewhere, that's the first law of thermodynamics.) Well, *FAT!SO?* has solved the mystery: The lost pound goes on vacation. It has a great time, and makes friends with other little pounds of lost fat. They globehop together for a while. Then they all come home, right back to where they belong, your hips and thighs.

Now there's photographic evidence of this process. Using a highly sophisticated, infrafat camera, *FAT!SO?* spies snapped these shots of little lost L. B. O'Fat during its world tour. L. B. loves to use the photos for postcards. You never know when you'll get a postcard from your pal, little lost L. B. O'Fat.

At the Sydney Harbor Bridge!

WEAR A MINISKIRT ON A HOT DATE.

Italy! Ciao bella!

I'm Little L.B., sittin' on the NYC Public Library steps. Grrrrowl!

Laissez les bons temps rouler! Cafe au lait and beignets in New Orleans.

Moi, je suis le petit pound!

There I am!

Hey, it's me! Little L.B., with Dave the cable car driver. He's got a nice belly, huh?

C'est romantique, non? Notre Dame Cathedral, the Seine, and me, Little L.B.

27

TRY ON ALL THE CLOTHES YOU NORMALLY PASS UP BECAUSE YOU THINK YOU'RE TOO FAT TO LOOK GOOD IN THEM.

THE *FAT!SO?* MANIFESTO

1 *FAT!SO?* CALLS FOR REVOLUTION. THE REVO-lution starts with a simple question: You're fat! So what?

2 There's nothing wrong with being fat. Just like there's nothing wrong with being short or tall, black or brown. These are facts of identity that cannot and should not be changed. They are birthright. They are heritage. They're beyond cures or aesthetics. They provide the diversity we need to survive.

3 Fat people are not, by definition, lazy or stupid. People who believe in such stereotypes, however, are.

4 *FAT!SO?* proclaims 12:01 A.M., January 1, to be International Fat-Outing Minute! During this minute, round folk are called upon to stand before their mirrors, smile, and proclaim, "I am fat!" The zealous will then gaze deeply into the eyes of their round loved ones and say, "You are fat, too!" Then, fat folk everywhere will applaud and blow noisemakers for a second time in as many minutes. Instead of starting the new year with yet another resolution to lose weight on some harmful, ineffectual diet, we'll begin each year with an honest moment and some relief from body-related anxiety.

5 *FAT!SO?* invites *you* to become a flabulous fatso—everybody, size 6 to 16, size 2X to 12X—because fat or thin, straight or gay, male or female, we have all at some point wasted our precious moments on the planet worrying about how we look. Stop that! Just say the magic words: "Yes, I am a fatso!" Write it here:

_____

With these words, you create revolution. You turn fat hatred back on itself. As a fatso, you possess the ultimate weapon against weight worries, body prejudice, and size-related discrimination: fat pride.

6 Practice saying the word *fat* until it feels the same as *short, tall, thin, young,* or *old.* Chat with your fat. Give it pet names. Doodle *fat* on your notepad during meetings: fat **FAT** fat fat FAT. Use the word *fat* with your parents, with your partner. Let friends in on your secret. Say, "By the way, I'm fat." You're not overweight, not plump, not bloated. You're fat! Combine the word *fat* with other words in new and unusual ways: sexy fat, fat and fabulous, fat pride. Use *fat* in a sentence: "You're looking good. Are you getting fat?" "I met a handsome fat man the other day." "Gee, I wish I could be fat like her." Try out these radical phrases on people you meet and watch their stunned reactions.

7 Large, big-boned, overweight, chubby, zaftig, voluptuous, Rubenesque, plump, and obese are all synonyms for fear.

8 List the five people you most admire.

1. _____

2. _____

3. _____

4. _____

5. _____

How many of them are fat? Is this more than you expected? Less than you hoped? What does your admiration really mean?

9 Fat is a numbers game. You tell yourself, "I could never weigh more than 140 pounds" (or 160 pounds or 200 pounds or more). If you exceed this imaginary limit, your body becomes an impossibility. When I weighed 160 pounds, I thought I was too fat for words. Then I went up to 200 pounds. The unthinkable had

happened. Now that I weigh 270 pounds and have friends twice my size, I realize that this numbers game is no different from the flat-world theory: We set weight horizons beyond which we expect to fall off the face of the earth. But the world is round, and all bodies are possible, acceptable, real.

10 FAT!SO? calls on all people every-where to stop lying about their weight, especially on driver's licenses. This self-hating practice reinforces the oppression of fat people and undermines fat pride. When Gloria Steinem turned forty, people kept telling her she didn't look it. She would patiently exlain that she did, too, look forty, but that women have lied about their age for so long that we think forty really looks like thirty-two, and that thirty-two should pass for twenty-eight. Likewise, people have lied about their weight for so long that we don't know a good-looking, 270-pound person when we see one. So what? So fat people can't get jobs, lovers, health insurance, or respect because our society can't imagine people weigh-ing more than the numbers on some bogus height/weight chart. Practice honesty right now. Fill in the following blanks.

My name is _____, and I weigh _____ pounds.

11 My fellow fatso, it's time we refused to be weighed during doctor visits. If a health professional pressures you to get on the scale, ask what possible medical purpose it would serve. A nurse said, "We need to track your weight so that, if it changes a lot from one visit to the next, we'll know, because it can indicate disease." Yeah right. Like I wouldn't notice a sudden loss of twenty pounds. Call the doctor's scale what it is: a tool of intimidation and humiliation, a means to justify the medical industry's antifat bias and diet-pill profiteering.

12 This is how we see: Vertical lines of thin bodies are good. Horizontal rolls of fat people are bad. It's a hierarchy of the Y-axis over the X-axis. Marx says: Reverse the terms, put fat on top. I say: Dichotomies are dumb. Love it all!

D IS FOR DEMAND

"Women's minds have been mutilated and muted to such an extent that 'Free Spirit' has been branded into them as a brand name for girdles and bras."
—Mary Daly, *Gyn/Ecology*

"If there is no struggle there is no progress. Those who profess to favor freedom and yet depreciate agitation are men who want crops without plowing up the ground; they want rain without thunder and lightning. They want the ocean without the awful roar of its many waters. This struggle may be a moral one, or it may be a physical one, and it may be both moral and physical, but it must be a struggle. Power concedes nothing without a demand. It never did and it never will. Find out just what people will quietly submit to and you have found out the exact measure of injustice and wrong which will be imposed upon them, and these will continue till they are resisted with either words or blows, or with both. The limits of tyrants are prescribed by the endurance of those whom they oppress."
—Frederick Douglass, "West India Emancipation" speech

TALK RADIO & YOU

FTER I'D BEEN PUBLISHING *FAT!SO?* FOR A while, I started getting calls from the talk-radio people. Those talk-radio people love an argument, and since Americans are brainwashed into believing that being fat is a bigger sin than lying to your mother, the national debt, and parking in handicapped spaces combined, they can always find someone to argue with me. Since I'm outrageous enough to believe that fat people shouldn't have to lose weight to gain respect, the arguments can get a bit boisterous—which is pretty much a talk-radio host's dream.

After I'd done a few of these radio shows, I started to feel like the target person in a pitching booth at the county fair: Hit the fat chick in the face with a tomato and win a stuffed animal for your sweetheart. As much as I love tomatoes, it wasn't my idea of fun. Of course, I used my best comebacks on the air. After each radio appearance, I'd get calls from all the wonderful fat people who heard me stand up for them and who couldn't wait to get hooked into the fat

community. So I kept going on the shows, hoping to reach people, despite the tomato factor. Then I started to see a pattern.

When the talk-radio host opened the phone lines, the very first caller would always say the same thing. (I started to suspect it was actually the same person calling in each time.) This caller, usually a woman, would use precisely these words: "I am so outraged by this woman. She cannot weigh 270 pounds and be healthy! You just cannot be healthy at that weight! It's not possible!" Then, if she was feeling extra helpful, she would scream, "Don't you know your fat is going to kill you?"

Wow. After hearing that several times, I found it really difficult not to laugh. No matter where the radio show aired, someone was always waiting to call in and parrot this message. What incredibly effective brainwashing.

Really now, these callers are not concerned about my *health*. That's the very last thing someone is concerned about when they take the time to call a radio station and scream at someone.

Here's what upset radio listeners so much. I had said, "I really encourage people of all sizes to eat well and to exercise. That's what I do, because I want to live a long, healthy life. I work out three times a week with a personal trainer, and I eat

31

my veggies. My blood pressure, blood sugars, and cholesterol levels are all normal. I feel great, and I weigh 270 pounds. I'm living proof that you don't have to be thin to be healthy."

Now, if someone came up to you and said gies. So far, it's working. All my numbers are normal, and I feel great." What would your normal reaction be to such a statement? The same as before: "Congratulations! Good for you!"

A normal reaction would *not* be, "You cannot

If everyone in the United States ATE NO MORE THAN 30 PERCENT FAT, the average lifespan would only INCREASE BY THREE TO FOUR MONTHS.

everything I just said, except for the part about being fat, what would your natural response be? "Congratulations" perhaps? Or, "Good for you. You sound like you really take care of yourself." But the minute I say that I am not trying to lose weight, that I have no interest in losing weight, the response of the average American talk-radio caller is to attack me vigorously and insist that, despite all of my healthy habits, I'm going to die, preferably sooner rather than later.

Now, just for a moment, even though I don't believe this for one second, let's just imagine that being fat really is some kind of killer disease for which there is no cure. Let's imagine that I go on the radio, and I say, "Hi. I have a deadly disease. But I'm doing everything I can to stay in good health. I exercise regularly and eat my veg-

be healthy! You have a deadly disease and you're gonna die! Nothing you do makes any difference. You're gonna die, die, die!" Even if fat really were the deadly condition these people claim it is, what kind of person would call the radio station to say that? To scream that? A hateful person, someone who wishes me (and everyone like me) dead, gone, disappeared.

Perhaps it's not quite *that* mean-spirited. Perhaps these angry people don't really believe that you can't be fat and healthy. They just believe—deeply, self-righteously—that you cannot be fat and get away with it. The very idea of me, a fat chick, enjoying life, getting away with it, sends them into attack mode.

I don't know why I was so happy when I realized this, but I was. Perhaps I was happy

32

because these callers were making my argument for me. They were demonstrating exactly the kind of hatred that fat people face in our daily lives, because what these callers were really saying was

1. Fat people make me sick. I can't stand the thought of you.

2. You shouldn't be able to stand the thought of you, either.

3. I deny myself the pleasure of food every day, because I can't stand the thought of being fat. How dare you not suffer as much as I do! How dare you eat a bite of something "sinful" and not beat yourself up about it the way I do! How dare you be happier than I am! If a fat person can be healthy without starving herself and working out obsessively, if she can be happy

for my health, they tell me they're doing it for my own good. Yeah right. They are trying desperately to put the uppity fat chick back in her place, and they want me to thank them for their efforts.

The "health" argument is a big old smokescreen for our old friend: fat hatred. When people realize they can't get away with expressing their prejudice against fat outright, they use the health argument instead, but the emotion behind their words is still hatred.

I realize that hatred is a strong word. Here's another way to think of it. Our culture currently believes that thin is good and fat is bad. This belief encourages the hatred of fat and the deification of thin. This belief is the basis for fat oppression and thin privilege. Now, no one person is responsible for this system of prejudice.

If everyone in the United States QUIT SMOKING, the average lifespan would increase by THREE TO FOUR YEARS.

without being thin, then I've suffered for nothing, and I can't stand that thought. I can't stand the thought of you (see #1).

When I point out the mean-spirited tone of these callers, when I ask them why they feel the need to yell at me if they are simply concerned

But once you become aware of the system, it's your choice, your responsibility, to choose how you will relate to it. You can reinforce it and try to benefit from it, or you can refuse to participate in it or live by its standards in any respect. It's a tricky choice, I'll admit. Fat hatred and thin

GATHER UP ALL THE CLOTHES IN YOUR CLOSET THAT DON'T FIT YOU, FOR WHATEVER REASON,
AND DONATE THEM TO YOUR LOCAL BATTERED WOMEN'S SHELTER.

worship are so ingrained and constant in our culture that most people are not even aware of these beliefs as choices. They seem like givens, fixed parts of the landscape. Fat prejudice is like a blind spot. Sometimes you can't see it, even when you're looking directly at it. (Radio callers don't realize they're being hateful; they really do think they're just concerned about health.)

The talk-radio hosts ask me how I can ever hope to change the world, how I can ever expect to end fat hatred. I can't. I don't. I do, however, hope to make individual people aware of this prejudicial system. I can't change your mind, but I can present a different angle on fat. From that angle, you might be able to catch a glimpse of the hatred that was hidden in the blind spot. Each person who sees the fat-thin opposition for what it is makes it harder for that blind spot to stay hidden, for people not to *know* when they're being hateful, for us to confuse hatred and coercion with health and happiness, and for fat oppression to flourish unquestioned.

Maybe that's why I'm happy, even though my realization about talk-radio callers revealed such hateful attitudes. I saw through that smoke-screen of alleged concern for the health of fat people, just like I've seen through the belief that fat is bad, and I won't be fooled again.

SHE LIKES IT!

by Boanne

'M A WOMAN, FORTY YEARS OLD, AND 183 pounds. The reason I don't think much about being fat (or at least didn't until recently) is because my mother was fat, both my grand-mothers were fat, and I had several wonderful teachers, both women and men, all through school, who were fat. The point is I suffered no lack of excellent role models who just happened to be fat. Most of the time, I don't think about being fat until someone else brings it up. Without even knowing it, my mother and grand-mothers, and my fat teachers were fat activists. They smashed all the stereotypes about fat peo-ple. They were intelligent, beautiful, active, vital, interesting people. I was slender when I was a child, but I would always say, "I want to be like Grandma when I grow up. She's so pretty." In my teens I got my wish and began to gain weight. It's very difficult to explain why I like being fat and how it makes me feel. Words like soft, warm, comfortable, earthy, and real all come to mind.

34

BUT WHAT ABOUT YOUR HEALTH?

T'S A REASONABLE QUESTION. AFTER ALL, I want to be healthy, you want to be healthy, everybody wants to be healthy. Duh.

But being healthy is *not* the same thing as being thin. A long life is not determined by a number on a scale. If it were, it'd be so great to be thin 'cause you'd never get sick, *and* you'd never die. Now, I am willing to grant thin people certain privileges—wearing lime green mini-skirts for the one minute they're in style, getting to date people like Donald Trump, being too small to donate blood—but immortality? I don't think so.

The question remains, though. What about all those dire predictions of death and disease for anyone who weighs more than a flight attendant? Isn't it unhealthy to be fat?

Of *course* it's unhealthy to be fat.

If you're fat, you're going to have a rough time getting health insurance. You probably won't get regular checkups and preventive care, and any health problems you might have (completely unrelated to your weight) will be a lot worse whenever you finally do see a doctor.

Even if you have health coverage, you probably avoid going to the doctor if you're fat. So you're in the same situation. Why do you avoid going to the doctor? Every time you walk into a doctor's office, the first thing they want you to do is step on a scale. Then you get the lecture, or the belittling remark, or worse, the weight-loss advice. You figure, as long as you feel okay, why risk it? You don't pay for abuse in any *other* setting, right? You value your mental health, so you stay away.

If you're fat and you do visit the doctor, he or she might decide to treat your weight, rather than your symptoms. You get a diet, rather than a diagnosis. The doctor says all your ills are caused by your fat. Six months later, you still have sharp pains in your heel or nasal congestion or shooting lights in your vision. So you find a new doctor. This time you actually get treatment for your plantar fasciitis or your sinus infection or your brain tumor. (These examples are based on actual cases.)

Your doctor may not like fat people. A recent study found that fat women are a third less likely to get breast exams, gynecologic exams, or Pap

35

smears. An exception: Fat and thin women get mammograms equally often. (The authors said that doctors may do exams more readily if they don't have to touch fat patients.) Fat women are at increased risk for certain scary cancers (breast, cervical, endometrial, ovarian). Getting less preventive care, researchers concluded, may "exacerbate or even account for" this increased risk. It's not the fat that kills us, it's the fat hatred.

If you're fat, you face discrimination in all areas of society, not just the doctor's office.

pressure cuffs to MRIs—might be designed to fit fat people, too. But isn't weight loss the same thing as wellness? you're wondering. Isn't it, after all, unhealthy to be fat?

I get asked this question a lot. So, even though I don't have a degree in science and am just a lowly health journalist, I scampered over to the local, world-class medical school and spent some time in the library there, catching up on all of the same studies that the medical handwringers and highly paid advice gurus are reading. I learned

1,200 CALORIES A DAY = STARVATION.

Studies have found that people who face even one incident of discrimination report more chronic health problems and depression than people who weren't mistreated. No research has been done to document the effect of lifelong mistreatment on the health of our ninety-seven million beautiful fat sisters and brothers, but that stress is there, and seeking medical help doesn't necessarily make things any better.

If the medical industry really cared about the health of fat people, doctors would be more interested in wellness than in weight loss. Their diagnostic equipment—everything from blood

some lingo, attended some conferences, and I actually came to distrust a lot of the long-cherished beliefs about the health of fat people.

Then, on January 1, 1998, the *New England Journal of Medicine* came out with an editorial entitled, "Losing Weight—An Ill-Fated New Year's Resolution." In it, the *Journal*'s editors, Jerome Kassirer, M.D. and Marcia Angell, M.D., refuted all of the same beliefs that I had come to question. Huzzah! So you don't have to take it from me. The chart at right lists all the things the *New England Journal of Medicine* itself says doctors don't know yet.

WHAT I'VE SUSPECTED ALL ALONG	WHAT THE *NEW ENGLAND JOURNAL* SAYS
We don't know why fat people are fat.	The editors caution against seeing fat people in medical terms "rather than as ordinary people who happen to be heavier than average, probably from some mix of nature, nurture, and choice."
We don't know how to make fat people permanently thin.	"Since many people cannot lose much weight no matter how hard they try, and promptly regain whatever they do lose, the vast amounts of money spent on diet clubs, special foods, and over-the-counter remedies, estimated to be on the order of $30 billion to $50 billion yearly, is wasted."
We don't know whether making fat people thinner will make them healthier.	"Even granting the existence of an association between increasing body weight and higher mortality, at least for younger people, it does not follow that losing weight will reduce the risk. We simply do not know whether a person who loses twenty pounds will thereby acquire the same reduced risk as a person who started out twenty pounds lighter. The few studies of mortality among people who voluntarily lost weight produced inconsistent results; some even suggested that weight loss increased mortality."
We don't know if weight loss *itself* is unhealthy.	"To add injury to insult, the latest magical cures are neither magical nor harmless."
We don't even know for sure that being fat is unhealthy.	"Given the enormous social pressure to lose weight, one might suppose there is clear and overwhelming evidence of the risks of obesity and the benefits of weight loss. Unfortunately, the data linking overweight and death, as well as the data showing the beneficial effects of weight loss, are limited, fragmentary, and often ambiguous."
We don't know whether the health problems commonly associated with being fat are actually *caused* by the fat, or whether they're caused by factors that go along with being fat, stuff like yo-yo dieting, poor health care, the stress of being targeted by prejudice, low self-esteem, prolonged exposure to double-knit polyester, and so on.	"Many studies fail to consider confounding variables, which are extremely difficult to assess and control for in this type of study. For example, mortality among obese people may be misleadingly high because overweight people are more likely to be sedentary and of low socioeconomic status."
We don't know the long-term health risks of dieting, diet pills, or weight-loss surgeries.	Actually, based on all the medical literature, we do know some of the long-term health risks of these practices. They should be enough to warn any sensible person to avoid them. Who wants to risk gall bladder disease, osteoporosis, lowered libido, depression, anemia, hair loss, weight gain, eating disorders, loss of essential nutrients, deadly lung disease like primary pulmonary hypertension, valvular disease of the heart, gangrene of various internal organs, liver failure, and death?

We don't know, we don't know, we don't know.

What we do know for sure is that there's a $40 billion diet industry in this country, and *its* health depends on Americans' desire to lose weight. If the diet industry can't hook you with their look-better-in-a-swimsuit argument, they're not above threatening you with poor health or paying a few "obesity" researchers to proclaim (based on data the *New England Journal* calls "limited, fragmentary, and often ambiguous") that being fat is a death sentence. Yeah right, *doctor.*

The *New England Journal*'s landmark editorial was accompanied by a study on body weight and longevity. In that study, researchers found no correlation between increasing weight and decreasing lifespan (in other words, the fat people were no likelier to die younger), with one exception. As obesity [*sic*] "experts" were quick to point out, the group of people in the study who were the fattest had double the risk of death. That's no reason to panic. This particular group of fat people had about a 5 percent death rate, versus the 2 percent death rate of the comparison group. That's hardly a death sentence. I'm tempted to say, "big whoop," and remind you that inequities in the health care of fat people (or any other number of factors) could easily account for this small variation in death rates.

Instead, let me put the statement that fat people are "twice as likely" to die into perspective. Medical studies will also tell you that men who smoke are *twenty-two times* more likely to die—from lung cancer alone—than men who don't smoke. (Which is worse for you? Being fat or being a smoker? How many people do you know who won't quit smoking because they fear gaining weight?) Per mile traveled, people who ride motorcycles are *sixteen times* more likely to die in a crash than people who drive cars. And people who live in Los Angeles have a death rate 26 percent higher than people who live where there's little air pollution. So what if you're a fat, hog-riding smoker in LA? Keep in mind that statistics that apply to groups of people are notoriously slippery when applied to individuals. There are no guarantees.

For fat people, I would argue that, beyond eating good food and getting regular exercise, skepticism is a key ingredient to health.

There can be no finer example of such skepticism than the work of Glenn Gaesser, Ph.D., a thin fellow and all-around nice guy who is an associate professor of physiology at University of Virginia and author of *Big Fat Lies: The Truth About Your Weight and Your Health.* Gaesser reviewed all of those medical studies about fat

EXPLAIN TO YOUR PARENTS AND FAMILY MEMBERS THAT THEIR DREAM OF A THIN YOU NOT ONLY HURTS YOUR FEELINGS,
IT ENDANGERS YOUR HEALTH *AND* YOUR RELATIONSHIP WITH THEM.

and health, and he came up with some startling insights into the popular beliefs.

✳ POPULAR HEALTH MYTH:

FAT IS A DEATH SENTENCE.

After reviewing all of the medical studies that tracked death rates and weight, Gaesser found that fully *three fourths* of them did not support the belief that the thinnest people live the longest. These studies either found that weight was not a very good way to predict how long someone will live or that, in some cases, the fatter people lived the longest.

✳ POPULAR HEALTH MYTH:

BEING FAT CAUSES HEART DISEASE.

First of all, there's a big difference between correlation and causation. But we can set aside that important point, because, as Gaesser's review of all the medical literature on this topic revealed, there is no correlation between body fat and atherosclerosis, the build-up of fatty plaque in the arteries. Clogged arteries are the leading cause of death for Americans, yet after more than five decades and tens of thousands of autopsies, the studies show that fat people are no more likely than thin people to have clogged arteries.

✳ POPULAR HEALTH MYTH:

BEING FAT CAUSES DIABETES.

Admittedly, people who get adult-onset diabetes are often fat. However, losing weight is not necessarily the answer for such people. Treatment centers have found that when diabetics improve their diet and exercise habits, they can lessen the severity of their diabetes and even normalize their blood sugars. These health improvements happen even though the people who change their diet and exercise habits don't lose any weight at all. (Gaesser cites such results from noted programs like the Pritikin Longevity Center and Duke University.) In fact, based on his review of current research, Gaesser says most people can rely on good diet and exercise to normalize such health problems as high blood pressure, high cholesterol, and insulin resistance—without losing any weight.

✳ POPULAR HEALTH MYTH:

STILL, FAT PEOPLE CAN'T BE HEALTHY.

My absolute favorite piece of research about fat and health comes from the Cooper Institute for Aerobics Research, the nation's leading authority on fitness. The Cooper Institute's ongoing study of a whopping 30,000 people has found that those who are the fittest live the longest,

WARN YOUR FAMILY THAT IF ANYONE TALKS ABOUT DIETS OR WEIGHT LOSS DURING HOLIDAY DINNERS, YOU'LL SIMPLY LEAVE.

no matter what they weigh. Fat people who exercise regularly live longer than thin people who don't. Or, as director of research Steven Blair says, "If you are a couch potato, being thin provides absolutely no assurance of good health, and does nothing to increase your chances of living a long life."

One other study about longevity is dear to my heart. David Weeks and Jamie James researched people who defy convention, in their book *Eccentrics: A Study of Sanity and Strangeness.* To their surprise, they found that eccentrics enjoy unusual longevity. So if believing that fat people can indeed lead long, healthy lives makes you eccentric, I say go for it!

✳ POPULAR HEALTH MYTH:

YOU CAN LOSE WEIGHT IF YOU TRY HARD ENOUGH.

By now, it should occur to you that this myth has little to do with concerns about health and everything to do with gaining thin privilege. In our culture, we currently believe that if you do everything "right" (spend hours in the gym; eat only brown rice, broccoli, and chicken breasts) that you will be rewarded with a so-called perfect body. If you can just achieve this perfect body, you don't just get all sorts of societal goodies, you also get the bonus of perfect

health. (And if you never step on a crack in the sidewalk, nothing bad will ever happen to you.)

A whopping 95 percent of the people who lose weight on diets gain back every pound within three years, according to a study reported in the *International Journal of Obesity.* Other researchers have found failure rates for diets as high as 98 percent. The NIH gives diets a 90 percent failure rate. A very few university-based diet programs have managed to document three-year maintenance of weight loss for 15 percent of their participants, but that's still an 85 percent failure rate, not great odds.

One researcher (who believes in dieting) decided to compile a database of successful dieters nationwide. Of the seventy-one million Americans currently on diets, only a few hundred are in this database, despite the fact that its definition of successful dieting is far from rigorous. To qualify as a successful dieter, someone may have lost as much as 100 pounds, and must have kept at least 30 pounds off for five years. That's a success? If I had gone through the extreme ordeal of losing 100 pounds, only to gain 70 pounds back, I don't think I would consider that endeavor a success in any sense.

Given that diets don't work, weight-loss zealots now claim that getting thin is just a matter of eating right and exercising. While those practices will indeed improve a person's health, they will not turn 270-pound me into 110-pound Kate Moss. Nor would I want them to. Healthy habits should not result in emaciation.

Faced with the failure of dieting, the public was willing to try diet pills like Fen/Phen. We now know these drugs had some serious and potentially deadly side effects. Diet-pill users risked death to lose, on average, only about 10 percent of their initial weight. Whatever new

surgery is a mutilation of healthy body parts. It is never justified. Besides, it doesn't work. In real life, most survivors of this surgery do not keep off whatever weight they lose. Often, the only permanent results are grim, lifelong side-effects, including dangerous and hard-to-treat vitamin deficiencies. When someone comes at you with a knife, the healthy choice is to get away from them as quickly as possible.

Why would any doctor recommend a treatment that fails 90 percent of the time? Why

You have a better chance of SURVIVING CANCER THAN OF LOSING WEIGHT and keeping it off.

drugs come out to replace Fen/Phen, I question whether the unforeseeable risks can ever outweigh the alleged benefits.

After trying diets and pills, some people, desperate to escape the mistreatment and hassles they face on a daily basis, decide to submit to weight-loss surgery. I really do understand why someone would consider this extreme option. The stigma attached to even the slightest amount of body fat can be daunting, and the surgeon's sales pitch can be very slick. However, as far as I'm concerned, weight-loss

would doctors persist in prescribing a treatment that is such a complete failure, when the health benefits of weight loss, and the health risks of being fat, are far from established? (Even the most experimental of cancer treatments are expected to have at least a 50 percent chance of success. And such treatments are only used on terminal patients who have no other options, not on healthy people.) Why do doctors feel justified in telling patients to lose weight when they know there is no known method of turning fat people into thin people? I can only think the reasons behind this weight-loss-at-any-cost mentality are a heady mix of money and fat hatred fueled, perhaps, by a thoroughly misplaced and misdirected urge to do good. (One "obesity" specialist at a noted university admitted during an interview with Sondra Solovay that his patients only have about a 3 percent chance of keeping any weight off. When asked why he would continue to subject them to prolonged starvation, given such odds, he said, "Maybe they'll be one of the lucky ones.") We should expect better from our health-care providers. The physician's oath says, "First, do no harm."

I realize that the information in this chapter goes against everything you've been led to believe in our fat-hating culture. But I don't think the conclusions this chapter offers are all that radical. I simply urge people of all sizes to eat right and exercise, and to stop worrying about weight. (Because worrying about your weight is, in itself, an unhealthy practice, and it can lead you to try things that are *really* bad for you.) Instead, hold on to a healthy skepticism. Hold on to your physical *and* mental health.

WHAT'S IN A WORD?

by Donna Marsh

GOT SICK AND TIRED OF BEING PUT DOWN FOR being fat, because, you know, I never thought I was ugly—ever. I just had to put up with all that garbage from other people. So I've been using the word *fat*, openly, and it works. I'm just myself again the way I was when I was five years old and didn't know I was *fat*.

FAT KILLS

by Betty Rose Dudley

DON'T LIKE DOCTORS. I DON'T KNOW MANY FAT women who do. My sister had cervical cancer. She didn't go back for her post-op checkup for over ten years.

I asked her, "Why? Don't you know this is dangerous stuff?"

"They're just going to tell me I'm too fat. I don't want to hear it. If I die, I die," she said. My sister works in a hospital.

I belong to an HMO. After a series of referrals, I ended up with this very young, very thin female doctor, obviously a jogger by the way she dressed.

At first it seemed as if this might be okay. She didn't hesitate to touch my body, and her touch was gentle. When the exam was finished, she said to me, with a smile, "Well, what are we going to do about you losing weight?"

"We're not going to do anything," I said. "I'm here because I can't get rid of this cough." She smiled, shook her head, and ordered X rays and tests. I thought, "Okay, fair enough." The next time I saw her she gave me a handful of weight-loss pamphlets, everything from Weight Watchers and Nutri-System to plain old calorie counting.

She said to me, "You should pick one. They're all pretty good."

"I told you, I don't intend to lose weight. I'm here because of a cough," I said.

"Don't you know that fat kills?" she said.

"I don't believe that," I said. "And I don't care anyway because I don't believe these diets work. These diets kill. Fat or thin, we are all going to die eventually, anyway."

"If you're depressed I can refer you to psychiatry," she said.

"No thank you. Just tell me about the X rays,"

"Oh, the X rays!" she said. "We have found an abnormality on your lung. It could be one of many things, including cancer."

By then I knew I needed a new doctor, but I couldn't change in the middle of this. It had taken me months to find this one.

I went back for the results of the further testing. The woman walked into the room with even more weight-loss pamphlets.

Now I was really pissed off. "Forget it," I said. "I have told you many times now that I am not interested in dieting."

She threw the pamphlets down on the desk, turned and put her hands on her hips and looked at me with disgusted disbelief.

"Well, I just don't even know why you bother to come here if you're not going to listen to what I say," she said.

"I came to find out if I have lung cancer," I said through clenched teeth.

"Oh," she said. You could tell she had forgotten. I did not have lung cancer.

I fantasize that I am a depressed fat woman, dying from unnoticed, untreated cancer, but intending to kill myself first. I will jump from the top floor of a high-rise apartment building near this HMO. I will do it early in the morning, waiting until this woman doctor jogs by underneath my balcony. I will time my jump so that I land right on top of her. The headlines will scream, FAT KILLS!

WEAR HORIZONTAL STRIPES.

E IS FOR EAT

"Taking food and drink is a great enjoyment for healthy people, and those who do not enjoy eating seldom have much capacity for enjoyment or usefulness of any sort."
—Charles William Elliot, president of Harvard University in 1896

"Let the stoics say what they please. We do not eat for the good of living, but because the meat is savory and the appetite is keen."
—Ralph Waldo Emerson, *Essays*

A HAPPY ENDING

by Dawn Falkowich

MY NAME IS DAWN, AND I HAVE BEEN FAT for my whole life. When I was ten years old I would cry to my mom and ask, "Why am I so big?" But now, five years later, at age fifteen, I accept the way I am, and if anyone has a problem, tough stuff, because I am perfectly fine. Some kids in high school will say something about my weight or body, and I just laugh and say, "Ain't it great! You're just jealous." I leave them standing there stunned. I'm not every guy's dream woman, but that is because they just don't know any better.

300,000

YOU MIGHT OCCASIONALLY READ IN THE NEWS that there are 300,000 fat-related deaths each year. Don't believe it. That number is bogus. You don't have to take my word for it. The *New England Journal of Medicine* said as much on January 1, 1998.

Actually, the *Journal's* editors said the 300,000 figure was "by no means well established . . . derived from weak or incomplete data" and suffered from "methodologic difficulties." (That's geek-speak for *bogus*.)

Laura Fraser exposed the logical flaws of this death threat in her excellent muckraking book, *Losing It: False Hopes and Fat Profits in the Diet Industry*. Evidently, the prediction was based on a previous study that tracked fewer than two hundred actual deaths (unrelated to smoking) out of the 115,000 women it surveyed. That's an incredibly small sample on which to base such a far-flung claim. Furthermore, proponents of the 300,000 figure failed to consider the health impact of poor exercise and eating habits. Such lifestyle habits "that tend to go along with obesity [*sic*] . . . may have contributed to the deaths,

GET ON TOP DURING SEX!

not the fatness itself," Fraser wrote. (Other research shows that fat people who exercise live longer than thin people who don't.) In other words, the prediction confuses correlation with causation. Anyone who eats well and exercises has little to fear, whatever their weight.

If that's not enough proof for you, the Advancement of Sound Science Coalition, a Washington, D.C.–based nonprofit group of scientists and former public policy officials, congratulated the *Journal* for questioning the 300,000 estimate. The group's executive director called the number "classic junk science" and "a misuse of statistics." Who would perpetrate such a fiction? And why?

Former surgeon general C. Everett Koop evidently needed a hobby to keep him busy during retirement. He started the Shape Up America program, with a little help (at least $2 million from Jenny Craig and Weight Watchers *alone*) from his friends, the diet companies. (I wonder what *I'd* be willing to do for $2 million. Hey, get Hugh Hefner on the phone . . .) Anyway, the good Dr. Koop got together with a handful of self-proclaimed "obesity" researchers (folks who don't mind accepting the occasional consultant's fee or grant from diet companies), and they discovered what we can now call, simply,

300,000. It's a multipurpose number. It doesn't just help the diet industry put some medically approved fear of fat back into people who wouldn't otherwise buy their ineffective product, it also comes in handy when diet pill makers needed to get FDA approval for nifty drugs like Redux (aka Public Health Disaster #1).

You see, the FDA might not have approved Redux back in 1996, but then Koop, et al., whipped out good old *300,000.* With so many fat people allegedly dying, Redux didn't seem so dangerous. The FDA approved the drug, and it made millions of dollars for its manufacturer, before they had to recall it.

This brings us to a disturbing coincidence regarding *300,000.*

The federal government now recommends that every single person who took flim/flam (excuse me, Fen/Phen) or Redux should get a painless but costly ($800) echocardiogram to check for heart valve damage. By conservative estimates, at least one million Americans took Redux alone (at least eighteen million people took Fen/Phen). Early reports that led to the recall of dexfenfluramine (Redux) and fenfluramine (or fen, its chemical mirror image) found that up to one third of the people who took the drug could develop heart valve problems. One third of one million Redux users is about . . . *300,000.*

Now we know that the 300,000 fat-related deaths are fictional, but the potential 300,000 health problems and early deaths caused by diet pills will be painfully real. As my Norwegian friend Ole Joergen Malm says, "Fat doesn't kill people; fear of fat kills people."

ANOTHER NUMBER

AS THIS BOOK WENT TO PRESS, THE FEDERAL government had just adopted new, lower cutoff points for "overweight" and "obesity." The result: ninety-seven million Americans—or fifty-five percent of us—are now fat. On the day *before* the government's ruling, only fifty-eight million people, or one third of us, were fat. (I'd say both numbers are too low. In a fat-hating culture, *everyone* is fat.)

These new cutoff points are supposed to be based on evidence of increased health risk. Here's the evidence that I find interesting: The government's data shows little difference in ill-ness levels for the *nouveau-fat,* and no decrease in their life expectancy, compared to people who weigh less. (Where did the government *get* these new figures? I know people who have more rigorous reasons for picking Lotto numbers.) A very small handful of white labcoat guys are setting these weight standards for the rest of the world. I betcha none of them has a friend who is fat, by any definition. But they do have friends in the weight-loss and diet drug industries, and those are lucrative friends to have. Here's an interesting coincidence: Under the new standards, someone who is 5'4" and weighs 145 pounds is now "overweight." Oddly enough, the average American woman (the diet industry's primary customer) is 5'4" and weighs 144 pounds. (Whew, that was close.) It must be nice, getting thirty million new customers in one day. The tobacco industry must be terribly jealous.

GET A HAIRCUT THAT DOESN'T "BALANCE" YOUR HIPS.

ANATOMY IS DESTINY

SOME PEOPLE ARE LEFT-HANDED, JUST LIKE some people are fat. In both cases, it's pretty much something you're born with. And in both cases, attempting to change one's fate demands constant and lifelong effort. Another eerie similarity: Being left-handed has even been touted as a huge health risk.

In 1991, the *New England Journal of Medicine* reported that left-handers die nine years earlier than right-handed people do. Nine whole years! This news worried lots of lefties—until flaws were revealed in the research and follow-up studies showed that being left-handed could shorten a person's life by two years, or eight months, or perhaps not at all. It makes one wonder whether the so-called medical facts about fat people's health risks aren't equally exaggerated.

The chart on the next page lists some other interesting parallels between fat people and our southpaw sisters and brothers.

So, what I want to know is this:

1. If being left-handed or being fat really is a health risk, does changing hands or losing weight do anything to diminish the risk? The *New England Journal of Medicine* said that some studies even suggest that weight loss increases mortality.
2. Or are these just cosmetic changes, designed to make people conform to societal standards, regardless of the health impact?
3. What if being left-handed doesn't cause any health problems at all? What if being *fat* doesn't cause health problems, either? What if it's just dangerous to be different?

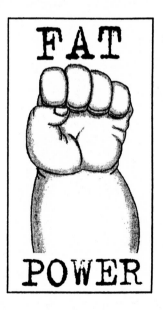

FAT POWER

GET A HAIRCUT THAT ISN'T DESIGNED TO CONCEAL YOUR "ROUND" FACE.

SIMILARITIES	LEFT-HANDED STUFF	FAT STUFF
Percentage of Americans	15 percent	55 percent
Advocacy/Support Organization	Left-handers International	National Association to Advance Fat Acceptance
Special Day	August 13, Left-handers Day	May 6, International No-Diet Day
Publication	*Left-Hander* magazine	*FAT!SO?*
Famous People	Babe Ruth, Jimi Hendrix, Harry Truman, H. Norman Schwarzkopf, Charlie Chaplin	Babe Ruth, Aretha Franklin, William Howard Taft, Alexander the Great, Orson Welles
The Cure	Rapping children on the knuckles until they write with their "right" hand (method discredited)	starvation diets, pills, surgeries, and ridicule (methods not yet discredited)
Negative Associations	sinister, illegitimate, evil, unlucky	gluttonous, stupid, smelly, lazy, ugly, undisciplined
Annoying Medical Term for It	sinistrality	obesity
Medical Explanation	genetics	genetics
Alleged Related Health Risks	five times more likely to die in accidents; also learning disabilities, migraine, depression, allergies, autoimmune deficiencies like rheumatoid arthritis and ulcerative colitis	the usual suspects: heart disease, diabetes, etc., etc.
Shorter Lifespan	between eight months and nine years	unestablished
Daily Annoyances	scissors, notebooks, screwdrivers, knives, power tools, oven mitts, school desks, can openers, cars, sports equipment, and computer keyboards, to name a few	clothing stores, turnstiles, airplane and movie seating, job discrimination, social stigma, and teasing, to name a few
Support Resources	businesses that specialize in lefty-friendly tools and other supplies	large-size clothing makers, fat-positive groups and publications
Cartoon Spokesperson	Ned Flanders	Eric Cartman
Natural Advantages	baseball, tennis, boxing, fencing, hockey, and a skill for adaptability	sumo wrestling, hugging, calming babies, holding cats, synchronized swimming, being a bodyguard or bouncer, and greater compassion

4. If our society disliked left-handed people as much as it dislikes fat people, would there be a $40 billion "righting" industry, instead of a $40 billion dieting industry?

5. If left-handed people were routinely discriminated against, would "sinistrality experts" take over from "obesity experts" in devising medical cures for social problems?

6. If being called "lefty" were as bad as being called "fatty," would little kids develop writing disorders instead of eating disorders?

7. If we really are "just concerned for someone's health," then why don't we harass lefties to change hands, the way we harass fat people to lose weight? Why don't we refuse to date or hire unruly lefties, the same way we refuse to associate with fat people who are "out of control"?

8. Why don't sitcoms make left jokes instead of fat jokes?

9. Why don't radio talk show listeners call in to tell left-handed guests that they simply cannot be healthy, that their attempts at self-esteem are disgusting?

10. Finally, why should a fat person have to compare her situation to that of a left-handed person, in order to expose the ridiculousness of antifat prejudice?

THE LITTLE BLACK DRESS

by Audra Spurlock

I AM IN TEARS AS I TYPE THIS. I HAVE BATTLED my weight for a long time, thinking that because I gained weight while I was pregnant, I could still get itty-bitty thin again, right? I have the most fabulous daughter, have gotten rid of the shitty ex-husband, have a good job, and I'm letting my *weight* get me down? Well, not anymore! I am proud of me, and that includes all of me. *FAT!SO?* has helped me realize that I am absolutely stunning in a little black dress and heels . . . at 225 pounds. I am fat, and I am *proud*!

DON'T WORRY IF YOU WIGGLE.

A LETTER TO FAT!SO?

by Bethany Johnson

REALIZE YOU DON'T KNOW ME FROM EVE, BUT I feel compelled to write anyway. I wanted to tell you what a difference you've made in my life. I've long struggled with my body, hating the fat that hangs on my frame and loathing the sight of myself in the mirror. Only recently have I come to accept my size and then, with *FAT!SO?*'s help, embrace it.

I used to wear clothes that allowed me to blend into the background, hoping that people wouldn't notice my misshapen body. Now I have a beautiful wardrobe that allows me to dress comfortably while looking terrific at the same time.

I've realized that every body is a work of art, and that an abundance of flesh is much more interesting and attractive than some coat-hanger chick. I wish more fat folk could see this, so that they may be able to stop hating their size and start enjoying their bodies. I love my fat, and I wouldn't lose it for all the chocolate in Switzerland.

THE CUTOFF POINT

F YOU WANT TO FIND OUT THE WEIGHT THAT IS healthy and normal for you, follow these steps:

1. Eat a moderate diet of good, nutritious foods (not a weight-loss diet). Have breakfast every day. Eat when you're hungry, stop when you're full. Don't subtract "illegal" food from your diet—add healthier foods like vegetables and fruits.

2. Get regular, moderate exercise three times a week for at least an hour. Exercise at your target heart rate. (To find that, subtract your age from the number 220 and multiply by 0.7. For example, the target heart rate for a thirty year-old would be 133 beats per minute. That's like a good brisk walk.)

3. Do this for the rest of your life.

4. Voilà! Your healthy weight is the weight that you can easily maintain while following steps 1 through 3.

Using this method, you might weigh more than what those height/weight charts recom-

BURN ALL OF YOUR "CONTROL" GARMENTS.

mend. You are, nonetheless, at your healthy weight. But don't take my word for it. This definition of healthy weight comes from no less an authority than Dianne Budd, M.D., assistant clinical professor of medicine at UCSF/Stanford

sent a standard for people of color or women or an aging population. That's not all that's wrong with the familiar charts. The convenient fiction of frame size also creates problems. When MetLife's head actuarial statistician,

---

During World War II, the Nazis determined that the MINIMUM NUTRITIONAL REQUIREMENT to sustain life in camp inmates at Treblinka was 900 CALORIES A DAY.

Medical School and attending physician at a UCSF Medical Center program called Women's Health Access. Dr. Budd is an endocrinologist, a specialist in the body's weight-regulating mechanisms.

What's wrong with the height/weight charts? These charts were developed using data from insurance companies. The millions of policyholders who contributed to this database were mostly white men who could afford life insurance. Their weight information was self-reported, whatever each man decided to put on his application, and no one tracked how each man's weight might change over his lifetime. At best, these charts could be said to represent the healthy weight for white men of a certain age and income level. They certainly don't repre-

Louis Dublin, first devised height/weight charts in the forties and fifties, the data showed that a broad range of weights yielded long life for each height. A person's weight could vary by thirty or forty pounds, without being associated with any greater risk of dying. (Again, this is based on data with the limitations mentioned above.) Dublin didn't like the idea of people feeling comfortable with a weight gain of thirty or forty pounds, so he invented frame size, to reduce that range. For each frame size, small, medium, or large, there would only be a ten- or fifteen-pound range recommended. That way, Dublin reasoned, people would start to worry if they gained five pounds. The problem is, there's no such thing as frame size. The original data set had no information about the alleged frame

51

size of policyholders. Ever since Dublin's little fiction, doctors have been looking for a way to measure frame size. They look at the length of the forearm, the circumference of the wrist, the thickness at the elbow. The vague ridiculousness of this quest may be one reason they're switching to the concept of BMI, or body mass index.

Let me report one last irony about height/weight charts, before getting into BMI. The federal government developed its own chart in the early nineties. Based on the government's data, the optimal weight ranges were the same for both men and women. For example, a five-foot seven-inch tall woman and a five-foot seven-inch tall man would both be advised to stay within the same weight range. However, the government's chart comes with this footnote: "The higher weights in the ranges generally apply to men, who tend to have more muscle and bone; the lower weights more often apply to women, who have less muscle and bone." This advice had no basis in the data and only reveals the bias, of someone in charge, that it's not okay for women to be larger than men.

As for BMI, it's just a number that represents your height and your weight and is quicker to say than "five-feet four-inches and 270 pounds." There's some little formula for figuring out BMI, but there's no point in repeating it here. If you're curious, I'm sure you can find out how to figure out your own BMI, but please don't mistake it for meaningful information about your health. The only way to determine your own, individual healthy weight is Dr. Budd's method, listed above. If you're really interested in numbers that say something about your health, try blood pressure, blood sugar levels, and cholesterol readings. Those are much better predictors of how healthy you are than BMI ever will be. People with the same height

She's not fat, she's just big-boned!

and weight could have radically different fitness levels, nutrition habits, blood pressure, blood sugars, and cholesterol numbers. They would have the same BMI, but totally different health profiles.

I just don't believe in a weight cutoff for health, or for basic human rights. I don't believe that it's helpful to establish such cutoff points, because they can only justify the practice of writing fat people off. The belief in a cutoff point gives medical researchers an excuse to look for a lucrative "cure" for fat people, rather than doing anything that actually promotes the wellness of fat people. Some people who eat well, exercise well, and live well are fat. They may weigh 200, 300, 400 pounds. Although you won't find them on any chart, or in a list of good versus bad BMI, those people are at their healthy weight. You may be at your healthy weight, too. Give Dr. Budd's method a try and find out.

F IS FOR FUTILITY

"I've been on a diet for two weeks, and all I've lost is two weeks."
—Totie Fields, stand-up comic

"If I had only understood twenty years ago the futility, the alienation, the self-denigration of trying to fit oneself into a mold. It was as if I was thinking of myself as a product rather than a person. I had yet to learn that the most incredible beauty and the most satisfying way of life come from affirming your own uniqueness, making the most of what you really are."
—Jane Fonda, *Jane Fonda's Workout Book*

G IS FOR GOOD

"And ye shall eat the fat of the land."
—God, Genesis 45:18

OH, YEAH?

LYN'S LASCIVIOUS COMEBACK

An ex-boyfriend once told me that I should lose some weight. I responded, "You of all people should understand that I am quite happy and satisfied to be in this body. It's a known fact that, when given the chance, you are too!'

—LYN SHEFFIELD

BONNIE'S BLAMELESS COMEBACK

Them: You've put on weight.
Me: (arms thrown wide) Yes! My genes are expressing themselves.

—BONNIE HAWTHORNE

PANDA'S PATENTED, PERFECTLY PRESENTABLE COMEBACKS

Them: Are you going to eat that? (referring to something like an ice cream sundae)
Me:
* I was, but I think you need it more than me. . . . Is it PMS, by the way?
* Yes, and anyone who tries to stop me!
* I *could* . . . Or it would look very good on your head.

When two people are talking about how fat you are, what you are eating, etc., get in their faces and say, "I may be fat, but I'm not hard of hearing." Then stay until they either apologize or leave.

—CLAUDIA STRONG

LORNA'S LACONIC COMEBACK

I was feeling down one day, and an acquaintance kept asking me what was wrong and pushing me to talk about it. So I said, "Despite popular belief, fat people are not *always* jolly."

—LORNA HOMMEL

SUSAN'S SASSY COMEBACKS

My top responses to strangers who corner me in restrooms and witness to me about Jenny Craig, or tell me what a knockout I'd be if I just lost some weight, or do that "shame-shame-shame" gesture with their fingers when they see me eat:

* Wow. Are you telling me there are actually ways to change the size of my body? Who knew?
* Do you really think I can maintain my shapely figure eating celery sticks?
* Thanks! And you'd look so much better if you'd wax—shaving leaves a stubble.
* I'm sure you mean well, but I just lost 150 pounds and I think I look great.
* You know, when my best friend was pregnant, she told me that total strangers would come up to her and put their hands on her belly. I always thought she made that up . . . but now . . . that wasn't you, was it?
* You're very brave to say so. Don't most people get rather hostile when you say such things?
* Yes, but then who would you have to feel superior to?
* You're kidding. I'm fat? Why didn't somebody tell me?
* A good therapist can really help you learn more socially appropriate behaviors. Would you like me to recommend one?

—SUSAN MILLER

RANDA'S RIGHT-ON COMEBACK

Them: How much do you weigh? (I haven't gotten this in many years, thank God!)
Me: A number far too large for someone with a single-digit IQ to comprehend.

—RANDA POWERS

HALEY'S COMMENTS, ER . . . COMEBACKS

Them: Hey, Lady, you're fat!
My reply:

* I know. It's great!
* Thanks for noticing. I'm not only fat; I'm also, smart, beautiful, and *employed*!
* So?
* Don't you wish you were too?
* I know. It was hard work, but I'm damned proud of it!
* You have some spinach or something between your teeth.
* Thank you. And you—you're, uh, well, *you're* a genius.
* And how! Want my secret? It'll cost you!
* Can I give you a hug?

And sometimes the best comebacks say something that makes absolutely no sense at all:
Pardon me, but do you have any Grey Poupon?

—HALEY HERTZ

ALAN'S APROPOS COMEBACK

Them: Three hundred pounds? I didn't realize she weighed that much. That's not possible!
Me: I didn't realize you were stupid, either, but your words betray you.

—ALAN BLALOCK

BOO'S BAWDY COMEBACK

I haven't had the chance to use this one yet. Occasionally, people mistakenly assume that I'm pregnant, because of my tummy. I'm dying to say, "Nope, I'm not pregnant—but, hell, the night is young!"

—BETSY "BOO" MITCHELL HENNING

CELEBRITY WASTING SYNDROME

A MYSTERIOUS DISEASE HAS STARTED attacking fat people who become famous. Poor Ricki Lake has a dreadful case of it. Oprah has suffered several bouts of this strange illness. And now Kathy Najimy of TV's *Veronica's Closet* is succumbing to what we shall call, for want of a more scientific diagnosis, celebrity wasting syndrome.

While both Roseanne and her former co-star John Goodman have battled courageously against the encroachments of CWS, other stars seem to have lucked out and achieved some kind of immunity: Tyne Daley, Aretha Franklin, Camryn Manheim, and Rosie O'Donnell, for example. This rare disorder can even jump from our world into the two-dimensional realm, attacking such well-known figures as the Pillsbury Dough Boy, the Michelin Man, and the lady who appears on-screen at the beginning of Columbia Pictures movies.

So little is known about celebrity wasting syndrome. Medical research is critical, if we are to save our talented fat celebrities from CWS. It's all too easy to overlook the ravages of this disease, just because its symptoms are socially acceptable. Meanwhile, our fat friends are shrinking away. And there's no telling where CWS will strike next!

(Note: We owe a debt of gratitude to Sondra Solovay, who first recognized this dangerous phenomenon.)

MY PERSONAL TRAINER CAN BEAT UP YOUR PERSONAL TRAINER

I F OPRAH CAN WRITE A BOOK WITH HER PERsonal trainer, I can certainly write a chapter with mine. Please don't misunderstand. Although this is the obligatory chapter on exercise, it is absolutely *not* the chapter on obligatory exercise. (That kind of thing is for high school gym class, infomercials, or branches of the military—places that rely on having a captive audience.)

Despite all the hoopla about fitness, most Americans don't get much exercise at all. More than sixty percent of Americans don't get regular exercise, according to the surgeon general's most recent report. How interesting. Fat *and* thin, Americans don't move around much.

You've heard all the explanations for Americans' inactivity: sedentary jobs, increased TV viewing, lack of leisure time, basic human laziness. But that list leaves out the most powerful reason of all: People don't go where they don't feel welcome. I'm betting that most people (at least 60 percent of us) just don't exercise because we don't feel like we look the part. If we don't fit in, we don't do fitness.

My personal trainer is Cinder Ernst. She's a sparkly eyed, size-14 dynamo. In the size-4 world of the gym, Cinder is considered fat. For years, she fought that label, working out obsessively and worrying about everything she ate. Despite her best efforts, she was never thin by gym standards. Looking back, Cinder says she always felt like she didn't belong.

When Cinder started her career in fitness, she started to realize that her dieting was not only motivated by dislike for her body, but that the dieting itself reinforced self-loathing. What's more, she realized that her workouts were often controlled by what she'd eaten that day, not by sound fitness principles. If she'd eaten a lot, she'd try to purge those calories on the StairMaster. If she ate junk food, she'd avoid the gym, thinking, "Why bother with fitness if I'm eating junk?" When she separated her workout from her eating and her worries about weight, an amazing thing happened. She says:

"I started to do only what I wanted to do in the gym—no workouts inspired by guilt, only workouts inspired by my preference. I was taking my cues from myself instead of from the opinions and judgments of other people at the gym. I didn't do the StairMaster for a long time."

It turned out that Cinder's self-directed, positively motivated exercise produced the kind of fitness she wanted, even if it didn't produce weight loss.

"When I started to normalize my relationship with food, I realized I also had to work on improving my body image. I've gone from not liking my body at all, to feeling neutral about my body, to liking my body sometimes, to liking my body more times than not, to liking my body all the time. Now I can say that I like my feet, my thighs, my hair, my cheeks, and my butt. I'm working on accepting my spider veins—I don't love them yet, but I've decided they can stay."

DON'T USE YOUR FEAR OF WEIGHT GAIN AS A REASON TO KEEP SMOKING.

In the process of breaking the connection between weight and fitness, Cinder became the kind of personal trainer and certified aerobics instructor that is, sadly, hard to find in most gyms. She's a personal trainer whose main concern is her clients' fitness level and joy in movement, not their appearance. She's part of a small but growing group of body-positive, nondiet fitness professionals. Her work with fat and thin clients is guaranteed to produce strength and endurance and also increased delight in movement and a happier connection to one's own body. Cinder says:

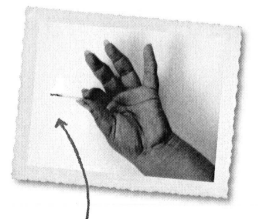

1 match = approximately .27 calories

"I can work with the muscle builders, and I can work with someone who hasn't been in a gym in years. Since I don't get clients by looking the part of a personal trainer, I really have to know my stuff. What I know is that our bodies adapt to whatever we demand of them. You hear fat people say they can't climb up stairs or do an aerobics class or walk long distances. Of course they can! I work with people on an activity until, gradually, they can do it. The more you do, the more you can do. I call it an un-vicious circle. Fitness isn't about looks or being thin. And you certainly can't tell how fit a person is by looking at them."

Increasingly, flabulous people like Cinder delight in breaking stereotypes by being both fat *and* fit. Instead of worrying whether they belong in a fitness environment, they adopt the true rebel's attitude: "Who says I can't?"

For example, Lisa Tealer is a certified aerobics instructor who weighs 350 pounds. She is also a co-owner, along with 200-something-pound Dana Schuster, of a fitness facility called Women of Substance Health Spa in Redwood City, California (half an hour south of San Francisco). Their gym is a haven for women of all sizes who want to take joy in movement and feel fit, free from the pressures of a typical health club. At Women of Substance, there are no scales, no calipers, no body fat calculations, and no admonishments about diet—just a friendly environment, fun classes, devoted clients, and a bowl of candies on the front desk.

I enjoy breaking the stereotypes, too. I exercise because it makes me feel good and because it's an investment in my long-term health. Being able to tell people (especially those irksome interviewers from the media) that I weigh 270 pounds, that I have a personal trainer, and that I work out three times a week is certainly a bonus. Take that, silly stereotypes! Of course, I'm also just keeping up a family tradition. My seventy-five-year-old mother is fat like me, and she still mows the half-acre lawn of my parents' suburban home every week. (With all that grass, she's getting an excellent workout.)

But our culture discourages most people from enjoying physical activity. In America, you're not supposed to go to the gym unless you already look like you go to the gym. You aren't fit to mountain bike unless you fit into those weird little black girdle shorts. You aren't supposed to swim if your aren't the Speedo type. You can't take ballet unless you look like you've got an eating disorder. And on it goes.

Researchers placed TWO FAKE PERSONALS ADS, one for a woman described as "50 POUNDS OVERWEIGHT [sic]" and the other for a woman described as a drug addict. THE DRUG ADDICT RECEIVED 79 PERCENT OF THE RESPONSES.

I think that's sad. The majority of us are disenfranchised from some pretty fun activities: biking, snorkeling, hiking, swimming, volleyball, and even aerobics. Pick one that *you* like. In a sense, we are disenfranchised from our own bodies, from using them to do any of the nifty stuff they're capable of. Why are we agreeing to this? How dare anyone say you should feel like you don't belong, like you're not welcome, like you can't be comfortable . . . in your own skin!

Sadder still, we're denying ourselves the feel-good effect and the health benefits that come from moving. The latest findings from the nation's leading fitness research center, the Cooper Institute for Aerobics Research, suggest that the biggest health benefit from exercise comes when people go from being sedentary to doing moderate exercise, about half an hour of physical activity three times a week. Contrary to our culture's zero-to-sixty mentality, you don't have to run a marathon to be healthy. Taking a walk, gardening, going out dancing—these are all perfectly wonderful ways to enhance your health and have a good time doing it.

Physical activity is not obligatory, but it is a basic human right. Don't let anyone—or any attitude—exclude you from places where you might enjoy exercising that right. Don't deny yourself the joy of spinning around with glee, rolling down hillsides, toodling around on your bike, playing tag with the kids, pumping weights, shaking your booty, hiking a hill, or any of the other thousand delightful forms of physical expression, just because someone somewhere might think you don't look the part. Follow some of Cinder's advice: Reclaim that feeling you had as a small child, feeling playful and alive in your body. The more of us fat rebels folks see on the move, the more we will indeed look the part. The more everyone will wonder why we (the 60 percent of Americans, fat and thin, who are inactive) denied ourselves for so long.

Oh, and by the way, my personal trainer probably won't beat up your personal trainer, as long as your personal trainer doesn't get in the way of people of all sizes enjoying physical activity.

FAT FITNESS RESOURCES

✳ **Cinder Ernst** offers personal training, fitness circles, and more!
(650) 738-1221
Web site: www.cinderernst.com
CinderErn@aol.com

✳ **Kelly Bliss**, M.Ed., provides size-accepting counseling by phone and offers *Fitness Plus* and *SuperFit,* the first nationwide video fitness classes including weekly on-line support groups: "Together we can work it out!"
(610) 394-2547
Web site:www.kellybliss.com
kellybliss@snip.net

✳ *Great Shape: The First Fitness Guide for Large Women,* by Pat Lyons, R.N., and Debby Burgard, Ph.D. (Palo Alto: Bull, 1990).
This wonderful book is full of important information and encouragement to help you enjoy movement at any size.

✳ **Women of Substance Health Spa**
363C Main Street
Redwood City, CA 94063
(650) 369-6626

My → personal trainer

CINDER SAYS...

What you think and say about your fitness is as important as what you do.

INSTEAD OF	TRY
Overweight	Large, fat, fit
Out-of-shape	Less active than I want to be
Should	Could
Adhere to a routine	Participate in movement
Weight loss	Health at any size
Willpower	Choice
Punishment	Pleasure
Feel the burn	Feel good

BREAK
THE CONNECTION

IF YOU WANT TO LIVE A LONG AND HEALTHY life, you don't need some fad-diet-guru-optimization-lifestyle book to tell you how, and you sure don't need *FAT!SO?* to tell you how, either. You already know the answer. It can be summed up in four words: Eat right and exercise. That's it. It sounds like no big deal until you try it and see how good it feels, how much energy you have, how your mood improves. Eat-right-and-exercise is powerful medicine. It's also the easy part.

The hard part, the part you will probably resist with everything you've got, the part that could turn your world upside down (in a good way) is the part where you stop hoping to lose weight. That hope has nothing to do with health or with living a long and happy life and even less to do with real hopefulness. Wishing your weight would change is about conformity and self-hatred and insecurity and prejudice, and everything that's designed to bring you down.

Now, when you connect the powerful force-for-good that is eat-right-and-exercise with the bottomless pit of negativity that is gotta-lose-

61

weight-and-be-thin, something has got to give. The way things look right now in our thin-obsessed culture, gotta-lose-weight is winning. Here are some of the ways that a desire for weight loss can destroy the benefits of eating right and exercising:

* You only eat right and exercise when you're trying to lose weight.

* You eat right and exercise for a while, but when you don't lose any weight, you give it up.

* If you do lose some weight, you stop eating right and exercising.

* You lose a few pounds by eating right and exercising, but not as much as you'd hoped, so you eat less and exercise more. You keep this up until you're in a real pickle.

* You think that eating right and exercising is only something that thin people get to do.

* You figure it's hopeless, you're always going to be fat, so why bother eating right, etc.

In all of these cases, worrying about weight comes first and healthy habits come last.

The real hope lies in breaking the connection between these two powerful forces. Focus instead on the habit that's guaranteed to be good for you, no matter what the number on the scale. Eating your veggies is always going to be good for you. Getting some joyful movement on a regular basis will always be good for you, too, whether you're fat or thin, whether you lose weight or not. Do these things because you love who you are, not because you want to make less of yourself.

"But," you're saying, "those things might also make me thin." Yeah right. And a gambling addict really will hit the jackpot, given just one more chance to bet.

You deserve better than that. You deserve the good food and the good movement and the good health *without* all the bad body messages tacked on. Don't swallow the poison pill. Break the connection!

H IS FOR HEALTH

"Adipose, while often pictured as a veritable Frankenstein, born of and breeding disease, sure to ride its possessor to death sooner or later, is really a most harmless, healthful, innocent tissue."
—Woods Hutchinson, the C. Everett Koop of his day, writing in *Cosmopolitan* magazine, 1894

"Our body is a well-set clock, which keeps time, but if it be too much or indiscreetly tampered with, the alarm runs out before the hour."
—Joseph Hall

WHAT HAS BEING FAT TAUGHT ME?

by Nicole M. Nicholson

'M AN ACTIVE COLLEGE SENIOR, SIX MONTHS away from graduation. I participate in two campus organizations and hold two part-time jobs. I carry nineteen semester hours. I design Web pages on the side. I am also a big, beautiful woman. When I started college, I was a size 10. I'm currently a size 22. My trip from there to here has been excruciating at times but also happy, and it is probably one of the fundamental things that shaped the person that I am.

As I was becoming fat, I learned to be more outgoing and friendly, for I found that I could no longer rely on my looks to attract friends and dates. Make no mistake—I am beautiful at any weight. However, becoming people-centered also made me more more confident. As a fat woman, I had to challenge the notion that it's not acceptable for women to take up space, to be noticed. Because of this, I have learned to be more confrontational, stubborn, and assertive overall. I find myself speaking up more. You could say that as I gained weight, I also gained a mouth, an attitude, and a spine. In addition,

becoming fat has finally taught me to accept my body as it is, as it was given to me—dimples, stretch marks, cellulite, and everything. I've learned to accept myself in a way that I never did when I was an awkward, skinny teenager. I realize that without that self-acceptance, others would be hard-pressed to accept me, too. Being fat has made me into a new and better me. Along with the size, I gained self-respect, confidence, and greater self-esteem. In this, I think my weight is not a curse but a blessing.

A TALK SHOW BY ANY OTHER NAME...

LOVE LURID TALK SHOW TITLES, ESPECIALLY when the topic is fat. So I researched a big list of them for the zine. I got the number for the *Maury Povich Show* from information. A harried assistant producer-type answered. In the background, I could hear four or five TVs playing at once, like the electronics department at Sears. I had barely explained what I wanted, when she told me to call another phone number and hung up. I called the other number. It was a weight-loss clinic in Los Angeles. Exactly what does a diet center have to do with researching fat-related talk shows? Thanks, Maury.

I finally located a transcription service that had a list of talk-show titles. I couldn't believe how many of the titles assumed that being fat is a bad thing. They would never make the same assumptions about race, or class, or gender.

Here are some of the titles I found:

* "When She's Twice the Woman You Married," *The Maury Povich Show*, October 9, 1991.

* "Fat Women Need Love Too," *The Montel Williams Show*, October 13, 1993.

* "Fat Myth: Can Fat Women Be Successful, Sexy?" *Maury Povich*, January 21, 1994.

* "Are Flight Attendants Too Fat?" *Jerry Springer*, April 13, 1993.

* "Fat Women and Families Who Hate Them for It," *Geraldo*, October 12, 1993.

It's funny how you never see titles like these:

* "Talk Shows: Sources of Prejudice and Stereotype, Empty Fluff, or Both?" *Jenny Jones*

* "Oinking Noises: Abusive or 'Motivational'?" *Richard Bey Show*

* "The Abdominal Six-Pack: Centerpiece of My Personality," *Geraldo*

* "If I Decide to Lose Weight, I'm Taking Everyone in America with Me!" *Oprah*

* "Make the Connection: Turning Self-Hatred into Best-Selling Books!" *Oprah*

* "When Being Thin Is More Important than Being Interesting!—or—How I Lost My Edge when I Lost Weight!" *The Ricki Lake Show*

WHAT CAN YOU DO?

KATHY BARRON WROTE THE FOLLOWING IN Hank's Gab Café, the discussion area on the *FAT!SO?* Web site (www.fatso.com):

I recently saw a list of one hundred reasons to lose one hundred pounds, things like, "So you can go swimming," or, "So friends won't be embarrassed by you." These aren't motivation to lose weight, they're motivation to hate yourself. I'm starting a list of things I can do. I'd like to hear from everyone, what can you do?

Gabsters responded with hundreds of fun things they enjoy doing at 250 pounds, 350 pounds, etc. Here are some of their comments:

At my weight, I can...

* Play co-ed softball and surprise everyone with how fast I am.
* Get dressed up and look glamorous and sexy.
* Run a business.
* Walk all over Disney World for 10 hours and do it again the next day.
* Be a wonderful, active, caring mother.
* Coach my child's soccer team and get voted best coach.
* Refuse to have friends who are "embarrassed" by me.
* Join a local theater group and get on stage.
* Have a healthy baby.
* Ride a motorcycle.
* Go topless at the beach.
* Fall in love and get married.
* Go scuba diving.
* Drive a cool sports car.
* Turn every head in the room.
* Comfort a child on my cushiony lap.
* Really enjoy every single day.
* Hike up to Manoa Falls on Oahu.
* Get high-powered job interviews.
* Run three to five miles a week.
* Have a handsome man buy me a drink.
* Swim laps at the pool for an hour and stop because I'm bored, not tired.

* Work full-time, care for aging parents, do volunteer work, and laugh with friends.
* Earn an advanced degree.
* Have a really hot sex life.
* Ski downhill, cross-country, and snowboard.
* Climb up escalators that aren't working.
* Carry a 27-inch TV up two flights of stairs.
* Throw a party for 200 people.
* Travel all over Europe.
* Go back to school.
* Be a vegetarian.
* Get a clean bill of health from my surprised doctor.
* Make other women jealous as I command the full attention and loving looks of my handsome husband.
* Shave my head.
* Have coffee with Jack Nicholson.
* Practice Tai Chi.
* Go horseback riding.
* Dance the cha-cha and have people applaud.
* Do everything I used to do 100 pounds ago!
* Do anything I damn well want to do!

Many thanks to Alia, Beth, Boo, Cathy, Cornelia, Daeryn, D.L., Heidi, Johanne, Kathy, Nalinie, Panda, Patia, Pippy, Robbie, Syndi, and Vik for the contributions.

START A SUPPORT GROUP FOR FAT TEENS. HELP THEM BE HEALTHY AND HAVE SELF-ESTEEM WITHOUT DIETING.

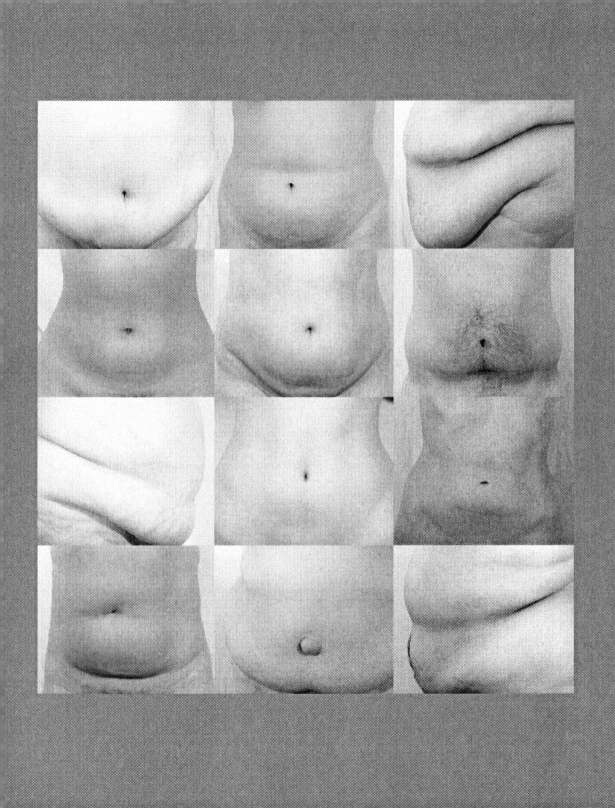

ANATOMY LESSON #2

THE BELLY

SELF-HATE CRIMES

WHEN MY PERSONAL TRAINER, CINDER Ernst, hears someone at the gym say, "Ugh, my thighs are gross," she walks up to them and says, "Hey! You just insulted your thighs. I want you to apologize to them." They laugh, but they do it.

never, ever tolerate from anyone else. How would you react if someone came up to you and announced, "Ugh. Your thighs are gross"? Surely your answer would *not* be, "Oh, you're so right. Can you ever forgive me for having thighs at all?" Surely, you would say, "How rude!" Or, "Get lost, jerk!" So the next time you catch that mean-spirited little voice launching into one of its rants, say just that: "How rude! Get lost, jerk!"

You also wouldn't let some stranger come along and starve you or make you take dangerous drugs. So why would you diet or take diet pills? You wouldn't let some stranger deny you

80 TO 85 PERCENT OF WOMEN fall into the category of "disordered eating"—people who ARE OBSESSED ABOUT WEIGHT and body image—at some point in their lives.

"If you could *hate* your body into changing, every woman in America would look like a magazine cover. Hating your body is futile, but it's especially futile around me," Cinder warns.

Despite Cinder's vigilance, and despite the best efforts of fat activists to make the world safe for thighs, people continue to commit self-hate crimes. We let that nagging internal voice say things about our bodies that we would

access to swimming pools or ban you from the beach just because your bathing suit uses more than eight square inches of fabric, so why do you deny yourself the pleasure of playing in the water? And if someone vowed to make you miserable every day of your life, unless you removed large parts of your body, you would consider that person incredibly cruel, wouldn't you? So why would you postpone your own hap-

BE A REBEL, NOT A CONFORMIST.

piness until you become thin? Stop being cruel to yourself!

Self-hate crimes are on the rise in this country. They're practically the national hobby. But you *can* arm yourself against them. Just ask yourself, "Would I take this kind of mistreatment from anyone else?" Or, better yet, "Would I treat another human being the way I'm treating myself right now?" If the answer is no, then that's a clue that you're committing self-hatred. Instead, practice this revision of the Golden Rule: Do unto yourself as you would do unto others.

THE SEARCH FOR THE CURE

THE FOLLOWING IS A HISTORY OF SUCCESS— the financial success of prescription diet-drug manufacturers, not the weight-loss success of their customers.

Keep this in mind: If any one so-called cure could actually turn fat people into thin people, then all the rest of these so-called cures would go out of business. The one true cure would make a lot of money for a little while, until all the fat people had disappeared. Then it, too,

would go belly-up. That's not what happens. The very existence of all these weight-loss potions is proof that none of them work.

Also keep in mind that the prescription drugs listed in this time line were sold to an eager public before their harmful, and even deadly, side effects were known. Sometimes drugs are sold to us *despite* knowledge of their dangers. Drug companies' customers are actually paying for the privilege of being guinea pigs.

Modern makers of doctor-prescribed diet drugs aren't looking for a one-shot cure for fat. They've taken a lesson from their colleagues at diet programs like Jenny Craig and Weight Watchers. They're looking for repeat customers. They want to find a diet pill that keeps you coming back, because that will yield long-term profits. Their dream pill produces a slight drop in weight (say, six pounds compared to placebo), a loss that only lasts as long as you take the drug. Sound familiar? One researcher gave it this spin: Fat is a chronic disease with no cure. So it needs ongoing treatment to prevent a relapse. (Does this remind you at all of the folks who want to cure homosexuality?) To all of this I say, "Yeah, right." That's why, as Americans keep getting fatter on average, the death rate keeps dropping. Nothing is wrong with being fat. Everything is

JUST SAY NO TO DIET DRUGS.

wrong with making a profit from the oppression and self-hatred of fat and not-so-fat people.

These days, though, the "cure" doesn't even have to work; people will still buy it. The weight-loss researchers now claim that people will see health improvements with only a 10 percent reduction in total body weight. They're just lowering the bar; the current crop of diet drugs only manages to produce a 10 percent reduction in weight. Being fat is no chronic disease. It's more like a chronic source of income for the diet industry. The bulge most likely to disappear is the one located in a fat person's wallet.

"Just Say No" to diet drugs. Say no to swallowing a little piece of self-hatred every day. Say no to being cut down to size by people who want you to feel bad about yourself.

Finally, please keep in mind: You can't put a price on pride. Fat pride is a whole lot cheaper than any of these alleged cures, and a million times more effective in increasing your happiness and even your health. Pride requires no prescription. It has no dangerous side effects and untold benefits.

"Medicine being a compendium of **THE SUCCESSIVE AND CONTRADICTORY MISTAKES OF MEDICAL PRACTITIONERS**, when we summon the wisest of them to our aid, the chances are that we may be relying on a scientific truth, **THE ERROR OF WHICH WILL BE RECOGNIZED IN A FEW YEARS' TIME.**"
—Marcel Proust

DON'T LIE ABOUT YOUR WEIGHT.

1780	1785	1790	1795	1800	1805	1810	1815	1820	1825	1830	1835	1840

A BRIEF TIMELINE:
PRESCRIPTION DIET DRUGS

In the last 100 years, literally thousands of preparations have been sold to Americans as weight-loss drugs. A history of the nonprescription snake-oils and over-the-counter placebos would fill a book. This time line chronicles only prescription diet drugs—substances that our very own doctors told us were safe and effective but which were, all too often, neither.

* 1893: THYROID EXTRACT

BRAND NAMES: Frank J. Kellogg's Safe Fat Reducer, Corpulin, Marmola

EFFECT: Weight loss is mostly in lean tissue, for example, the heart muscle.

POPULARITY: Kellogg's ads got over 100,000 inquiries.

RISKS: Osteoporosis, increased heart rate, palpitations, sweating, chest pain, sudden death

* 1936: DINITROPHENOL

USES: A benzene-derived shocking-pink dye, World War I explosives, insecticide and herbicide, weight loss drug

EFFECTIVENESS: Effective, but toxic

POPULARITY: Up to 100,000 people used it

RISKS: Skin rashes, cataract blindness, lost sense of taste, death by hyperpyrexia (exceptionally high fever due to increased metabolism). The body cannot process or excrete the drug, so it quickly builds up to toxic levels.

* 1937: AMPHETAMINES

STREET NAMES: Black beauties, eye-openers, uppers, speed

EFFECTIVENESS: Average loss of two to ten pounds before drug loses effectiveness. Weight regain without the drug.

POPULARITY: Two thirds of weight-loss patients in 1948 were prescribed amphetamines. In 1970, dieters consumed two billion amphetamine pills. It was prescribed to children until the seventies.

RISKS: Accelerated heart rate, increased blood pressure, palpitations, dry mouth, blurred vision, hallucination, tremors, addiction, withdrawal problems, congestive heart failure, seizures, and sudden death

* 1940s: DIGITALIS

EFFECT: Normally prescribed as a medication for congestive heart disease and heart rhythm disorders, digitalis increases the heart's pumping action.

RISKS: A very narrow range of safe dosage. With small overdoses, one possible side effect is loss of appetite. Not recommended for people with thyroid deficiency.

* 1979: PHENYLPROPANOLAMINE (PPA)

BRAND NAMES: Dexatrim, Accutrim, Dex-a-Diet, Diadex, Prolamine, Propagest, and Unitrol—all available over the counter.

ADVERTISING SPENDING: $40 million a year

SALES: Thompson Medical Co. made $1 billion in 1985 on Appedrine, Prolamine, Control, and Dexatrim.

TOLL: Poison Control Centers reported 47,000 complaints related to PPA use in 1989 alone.

EFFECTIVENESS: Undocumented and unknown

RISKS: Anxiety, disorientation, palpitations, headache, hallucination, insomnia, nausea, vomiting, a rebound effect of fatigue and hyperphagia (eating a lot), dangerously high blood pressure, abnormal heart rhythm, heart and kidney damage, heart attack, strokes, psychosis, and death

* 1994: FENFLURAMINE/PHENTERMINE (FEN/PHEN)

SALES: 60,000 prescriptions in 1994, 1 million in 1995, 18 million in 1996

PRICE: $50 a month, for life (more than the membership rate at many gyms)

EFFECT: An average 15 percent loss of body weight, as long as the drug is taken daily

USE: Off-label use. No FDA approval or long-term studies were required for this drug combo to be used as a weight-loss treatment.

RISKS: Heart valve defects, primary pulmonary hypertension (an often-fatal lung disease), withdrawal depression, schizophrenic behavior, possible brain damage

1935   1940   1945   1950   1955   1960   1965   1970   1975   1980   1985   1990   1995   2000   2005

* 1996: DEXFENFLURAMINE

BRAND NAME: Redux, by Interneuron Pharmaceuticals

EFFECT: Six pounds of weight loss, on average, when compared to a placebo

PRICE: $2.40 a day or $72 a month for life. *Business Week* estimated the annual market for diet drugs at $3 billion before Redux was removed from sale.

SALES: At *least* 1 million prescriptions during the year it was available

RISKS: The same as for fenfluramine

* 1998: SIBUTRAMINE

STREET NAME: Meridia, by Knoll Pharmaceuticals

PROGNOSIS: Approved by the FDA November 24, 1997. Became available in spring 1998.

EFFECT: Serotonin and dopamine re-uptake inhibitor

USE: For life. People who discontinue use regain weight faster than they would if they had stopped dieting.

EFFECTIVENESS: Ten to fourteen pounds average loss in the first year of use

RISKS: Increased heart rate, dangerous increases in blood pressure. (Wasn't that something that weight loss is supposed to *prevent*?)

* 1998: ORLISTAT

STREET NAME: Xenical, by Hoffman LaRoche

PROGNOSIS: Tied votes in the FDA advisory committee in March 1998. (In 1997, the approval process hit a serious snag when the company disclosed disturbing and unexpected findings of increased breast cancer rates for people who used the drugs in test runs.)

EFFECT: Lipase inhibitor. (Prevents your body from absorbing one third of the fat in foods that you eat.)

RISKS: Vitamin deficiencies, fecal urgency, anal leakage, smelly and greasy stools, unexplained link to breast cancer

COMING SOON

At least twenty more weight-loss drugs are in development right now, in a race for the billion-dollar market in fat shame.

73

THE SAME OLD SONG

Here's a ditty to hum to yourself the next time the FDA approves a magic pill.

(Sung to the tune of "Oh My Darlin' Clementine.")

by Netta Smith

To a local diet doctor
Who said only thin was fine
Went a young miss
Seeking thinness
And her name was Clementine.

Chorus:
Oh my darlin', oh my darlin'
Oh my darlin' Clementine,
You are lost and gone forever.
Dreadful sorry, Clementine.

She was healthy, strong, and
   lovely,
And she wore a dress size nine.
But she thought that
She was so fat
And for thinness she did pine.

Chorus

Magic pills, the doctor told her,
Soon would make her look
   divine.
So she took them
And she got thin.
But she missed the warning signs.

Chorus

Her poor heart just couldn't
   take it
As she withered on the vine.
She's a size three—
What a vict'ry!
But she's dead at twenty-nine.

Oh my darlin', oh my darlin'
Oh my darlin' Clementine,
You are lost and gone forever.
Dreadful sorry, Clementine.

GET A TATTOO THAT SAYS, "BORN TO BE WIDE!"

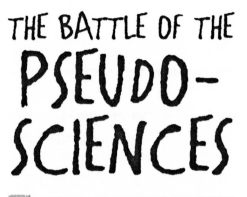

THE BATTLE OF THE PSEUDO- SCIENCES

THE HUMAN MIND WORKS IN FUNNY WAYS. One night I was watching a documentary on bariatric medicine—that branch of medicine devoted to the study of my people, or what scientists call "obesity." As I was watching, it struck me that the so-called science of weight management bears some eerie similarities to another so-called science, that of phrenology.

In phrenology, a science that was wildly popular 150 years ago, practitioners of the art would use calipers to measure various bumps and bulges on a person's skull. They thought that the brain was divided into organs of character, and that these brain structures shaped the surface of the skull. A large organ of, for example, empathy, would result in a bump in the corresponding area of the noggin. Measurements of these bumps produced a complicated chart, a map of the subject's char-

acter. (Unlike bariatric medicine, phrenology is now discredited as a pseudoscience.)

The particular scene in the movie that so inspired me depicted a person in a white lab coat using calipers to measure the flesh of a fat person's body. The technician marked random points all over the fat person's back and torso with a wide black felt-tip. Then he applied the calipers to the marks, squeezing the calipers' bowed tips together until the fat person protested that really, honestly, that was enough. After each pincer grab, the white-lab-coated person wrote down a measurement on a little chart. Sounds familiar, huh?

The Puritans put PEOPLE IN THE STOCKS FOR HAVING SPICE in their KITCHENS.

Here are some other striking similarities I noticed between phrenology and bariatric medicine: Both fields make judgments about people based on the shape and size of their anatomy, either the head or the hips. Practitioners of both sciences are quite happy to make a diagnosis based on a quick visual assessment of the

WHEN YOU'RE OUT AT A NICE RESTAURANT, GO AHEAD AND ORDER THE DESSERT.

Fat women are **TWICE AS LIKELY TO ENJOY SEX AND TO REACH ORGASM,** compared to thin women, according to a survey conducted by <u>Weight Watchers</u> magazine. **(A FULL 85 PERCENT** of fat women surveyed said they enjoy sex, compared to only 40 to 45 percent of thin women who said they did. And 70 percent of fat women said they almost always have orgasms, compared to just 29 percent of thin women.) Fat women were also **TWICE AS LIKELY TO BE HAPPY WITH THEIR PARTNERS** and their relationships. Three fourths of the fat women surveyed said their partners found them **ATTRACTIVE AT THEIR PRESENT WEIGHT.**

patient. (Phrenological and bariatric diagnoses alike can be made based only on a photograph, or relatively accurate drawing of the patient.) And both sciences have announced new "break-throughs" that received the kind of immediate, enthusiastic, near-hysterical, nationwide public attention that is usually reserved for the release of a new batch of Beanie Babies or a new Riverdance video.

Both sciences offer supplicants a kind of self-discovery. People enjoy receiving a phrenological or bariatric analysis of themselves, in the same way they might enjoy reading their horo-scope or consulting a 900-number psychic. In the 1800s, people lined up at Coney Island, and at county fairs across the nation, to receive phrenological interpretations of their skulls. Phrenologists even devised a complicated hood mechanism that descended over a person's head and performed all the necessary mea-surements quickly and accurately. Likewise, people nowadays line up in shopping malls and health clubs to have their body fat content ana-lyzed by various ingenious devices.

The definition of both a phrenologist and a bariatric physician is largely determined by the

TAKE A BRISK WALK (BECAUSE IT FEELS GOOD, NOT BECAUSE IT'LL BURN CALORIES).

fact that the practitioner pays annual dues to the corresponding professional organization. (In addition to having a medical degree and holding a valid license to practice medicine, bariatric physicians simply pay $395 in annual dues and perform a modicum of continuing education units each year. There is no residency program in bariatric medicine. Doctors who wish to claim board certification must pass an eight-hour exam, but this test is not required to be a bariatrician.)

On the level of ideology, both phrenologists and bariatric physicians believe that social ills can be addressed with medical or scientific cures. Bariatric physicians are the first to admit that fat-related discrimination is rampant in our society. Instead of fighting to reverse that prejudice, bariatricians perform surgeries or liposuction to combat the fat itself. Phrenologists performed a similar service for the bigots of their day, justifying racism by means of their science, since, they argued, the cranial profiles of black people were more slanted than the cranial profiles of white people. Anthropometry is evidently destiny, according to both phrenology and bariatric medicine.

In their day, phrenologists believed that a thorough analysis of the skull could yield information that would help the patient regulate every area of his or her life, from vocation and marriage to the reduction of crime and mental illness. Similarly, bariatric physicians often agree with their patients' belief that becoming thin will solve virtually all of their problems in life. In fact, both sciences are based on a firm belief in human perfectibility. It is therefore understandable if the practitioners of both phrenology and bariatric medicine not only take it upon themselves to define human physical perfection but also serve as models for these standards, since they are, quite often, thin white men with high brows.

It is a pitfall of scientific inquiry that seemingly objective data may be interpreted to conform to the exact contours of the scientist's personal belief system. For example, here are phrenological analyses of two famous people of bygone days, as published in the *Phrenological Journal.* About Susan B. Anthony, the phrenologists of her day wrote, "Is she a womanly woman? . . . certainly not." Of Frederick Douglass, they said, "He is a natural worker, and could not live a passive, idle life." These conclusions reveal more about the analyst's attitudes on gender and race than they reveal about Ms. Anthony or Mr. Douglass. One wonders if bariatricians, like

77

phrenologists before them, might not indulge in a similarly prophetic science, reading their own psychological predispositions and social context regarding fat people into their seemingly objective data.

As Stephen Jay Gould explains in his brilliant book on scientific racism and IQ testing *The Mismeasure of Man:*

An old tradition in science proclaims that changes in theory must be driven by observation. Since most scientists believe this simplistic formula, they assume that their own shifts in interpretation only record their better understanding of newly discovered facts. Scientists therefore tend to be unaware of their own mental impositions upon the world's messy and ambiguous factuality. Such mental impositions arise from a variety of sources, including psychological predisposition and social context.

Although phrenology is now considered quackery, it did serve as the jumping-off point for two valuable fields of modern inquiry: psychoanalysis and the neurosciences. Likewise, bariatric medicine may yet inspire humanity to produce a science that answers our basic questions about fat: What makes people fat? What makes people thin? What does our intense interest in the answers to these questions say about us? And most importantly, does the shape of someone's body, any more than the shape of their skull, say anything at all about their health, their happiness, or their value as a human being?

❙ IS FOR ❙NEVITABLE

"Who ever hears of fat men heading a riot, or herding together in turbulent mobs?"
—Washington Irving, *Knickerbocker's History of New York*

SKEPTICAL BUT EQUAL

JUST FOR GIGGLES ONE DAY, I DECIDED TO see if there were any medical studies about the health risks of height, since I was getting pretty tired of all those conflicting reports about the health risks of weight.

What do you know? Short people have more health problems than tall people do.

In a 1989 study of 12,000 Swedish people, the shortest Swedes were 20 percent more likely to die than the tallest Swedes. In 1992, a study of

50,000 Swedish men found that guys who were five-feet four-inches tall or shorter had *double* the death rate of Swedes of average height.

In both of these studies, however, researchers didn't blame the short men for their health problems. Nor did they recommend heightening diets, height pills, or height-gain surgery. Instead, they said that social and economic background accounted for most, if not all, of the increased health risk the short men faced. In one study, the researchers made a point of comparing height to weight and said that, based on their findings, *weight seems to be much more determined by genetics than height is.* (In fact, 80 percent of a person's weight is genetically determined, according to a 1986 study of identical twins reported in the *Journal of the American Medical Association.*)

Yet in 1997, researchers looked at thirty years worth of data on a group of middle-aged men who were all at the same socioeconomic level. They reported that every two-inch increase in height was associated with an 18 percent decrease in the risk of dying from heart disease. So one is left to wonder whether being short causes any health problems at all, or whether it is simply correlated with life conditions that tend to cause health problems.

Please understand, I have nothing against short people. I'm five-feet four-inches tall, after all, and I'm certainly not trying to make a case *against* being short or being fat. I'm just interested in the remarkable lack of hysteria in the reports on height and health risk, when similar findings about weight would generate widespread media alarm and renewed interest in weight loss. I'm also impressed by the researchers' willingness to look at social factors that might cause health problems for short people, rather than blaming the height difference itself. It makes me wonder why researchers who study weight are so quick to discount the social and economic realities that affect fat people. Could it be that it's easier to package and sell weight loss than it is to package and sell an end to discrimination?

Here are some facts: Since 1960, the average American has gotten two inches taller. This increase in American height is evidently so little cause for alarm that most people aren't aware of it. In the last ten or fifteen years, Americans have also gained about eight pounds, on average. You've certainly heard of that little fact, since our increased weight—unlike our increased height—is portrayed as a cause for serious alarm.

BASE YOUR FRIENDSHIPS ON ANYTHING BUT DIET TALK.

At the same time that Americans have been gaining height and weight, we have also lowered cholesterol levels, reduced heart disease, and markedly increased our life span. We are fatter than ever, and we're also living longer, healthier lives than ever before.

Or at least some of us are. The Centers for Disease Control came out with a report about the health of African Americans in early 1998. The report showed that despite social and economic improvements in the last thirty years, black people do not enjoy the same health or life span as white people do—and that disparity may be increasing, rather than decreasing.

that race, discrimination, and social and cultural factors influence the care people receive and, consequently, their health."

Again, please don't misunderstand me. I am not stunned in the slightest by the idea that racism affects the health and health care of African Americans. I am stunned that top officials are willing to admit it. Perhaps I get a vicarious thrill from this admission, trying to imagine what it will be like when the U.S. surgeon general admits that fat people are in poorer health than thin people, not because body fat is some kind of deadly substance but because there is widespread prejudice against us in the medical system.

Question: How much does the AVERAGE FAT WOMAN EARN EACH YEAR, compared to her thin peers? ANSWER: NEARLY $7,000 LESS.

For example, since 1980, the number of diabetes cases among black people increased by 33 percent, an increase three times greater than that among white people. Black people live to about age seventy, compared to age seventy-six for whites. The stunning conclusion from federal health analysts, as reported in *The New York Times*, is that there is "growing evidence

Randall Morgan, M.D., an orthopedic surgeon and a former president of the predominantly black National Medical Association, was quoted by *The New York Times* as saying, "We have a two-tiered health care system."

Indeed we do. Like black people, fat people are relegated to the second tier. We have to live, and die, with the consequences of that.

J IS FOR JIGGLE

"Being thin isn't normal. It's just common."
—Paraphrase of filmmaker Derek Jarman, who actually said that *heterosexuality* isn't normal, just common. From his 1992 memoir, *At Your Own Risk*.

"We contrive to keep calories down and feel triumphant when we get compliments on a low-calorie meal from the man we're trying to please."
—Lady Bird Johnson, former first lady

THE SOAP LADY

by Lynn McAfee

IN 1971, I WAS WORKING AS A PAGE IN THE medical library at the College of Physicians of Philadelphia. It's an old club from the 1700s that doctors pay a lot of money to join. They have a building with big marble staircases. The Mütter Museum, a collection of odd specimens, was downstairs. We would go there during our lunch hour. There was one room we called the pickled baby room.

One specimen was called the Soap Lady. One day we were talking to the curator, asking her what it was. She told us that there had been a very fat woman who died during a plague and was put in a mass grave. Because of the moisture and the soil conditions, her fat had turned into soap. The Soap Lady had been preserved in a coffinlike thing with a window in the top. You could make out that she was a person, but her flesh was really dark like pitch. The curator told us that at the turn of the century, some doctors in leadership at the college got drunk one night. They broke off a piece of this woman's remains and used it as soap to see how it lathered.

I was horrified. I knew that my doctors saw me as a freak, not a person. At the time, I had just started to understand that diets don't work. I was starting to ask why doctors didn't tell people that dieting didn't work. And that story just said it all. That they could take such a disrespectful attitude toward a fat body! That's not okay.

I've dedicated my life to making sure that medical treatments for fat people are respectful and safe. I've lobbied the FDA and the NIH about weight-loss drugs. I've educated doctors about the discrimination fat people face in medical settings. I've done fat-related sensitivity training in the pharmaceutical industry. I just want to make sure that they don't get away with treating us the way they treated the Soap Lady ever again.

DEVOTE A SHELF OF YOUR LIBRARY TO FAT-POSITIVE BOOKS, WHERE VISITORS WILL BE SURE TO NOTICE.

BEATING A HORSE OF A DIFFERENT COLOR

YOU'LL OFTEN HEAR SOMEONE SAY, "IT'S MY fault that I'm fat." Well, you know what? It's my fault I'm white. It really is.

If I cared about myself, I'd do something about this disgusting pallor. I don't get as much like me could do something about our white problem if we really wanted to. We should happily undergo the burning and the peeling and the risk of skin cancer, in order to achieve the obvious social and health benefits of darker skin. If white people had any willpower or self-respect, we simply wouldn't mind the pain.

The white-loss industry offers a variety of cures, although they no longer get away with promising total melanin enhancement. (Too many people have gone through the heartache of white loss, only to regain their natural lightness in a matter of months.) The industry admits that, at best, their products produce about a ten percent increase in attractive, healthy-looking skin color. People go for it

---

Average number of POUNDS GAINED by each American DURING THE LAST TEN YEARS: EIGHT.

---

sun as I should. I love the indoors, and spend far too much time in the shade. When I do go outside, I have deep cravings for sunblock, the higher the SPF the better. (I confess to indulging in this guilty pleasure all to often. I just can't stop myself from slathering it on.)

Most medical experts agree that pale people because they're so desperate for darker skin.

A few renegade health professionals claim that skin color is genetically determined, and that there's nothing wrong with being white. They even cite a handful of studies as proof of their unusual stance. However, as far as mainstream public opinion goes, pale folk are supposed to hate their skin, and be willing (even eager) to do anything to lose white. Because even losing a little bit of white would make white people look and feel better.

The fashion industry, the advertisers, and the media would have the public believe that only brown-skinned women are beautiful. Call me crazy, but despite everything, I think I look just fine with white skin. I even wear sleeveless clothes, and sometimes shorts. People tell me to cover up, to wear something more appropriate for someone my color, but I like the way I look. I'd probably get more dates if I were darker, but I would always wonder if they only liked me because of my skin.

Since I've decided that white can be beautiful, I actually enjoy getting naked with lovers, instead of dreading it. On the job, I manage to avoid discrimination by working for people who appreciate the skill it takes to live successfully as a pale person. In the end, I'm white. I don't care if it's my fault or not. I'm going to do everything I can to live a happy, healthy life.

FAT IS NOT A CLOAKING DEVICE!

F YOU'RE FAT, FOLKS THINK THEY KNOW THINGS about you. Sometimes they will come right up to you and tell you these things. Other times, they will just think these things to themselves, like a tune that gets stuck in their heads. These things are what I like to call assumptions. And these particular assumptions are based in the bedrock belief that it's bad to be fat. But since this is belief and not fact, we could just as easily believe the opposite, that it's perfectly okay to be fat, which would mean that all sorts of annoying assumptions get turned inside out.

* ASSUMPTION: If you're fat, there's a thin person inside you.

NEW VERSION: And if you're thin, perhaps one day you'll realize your true fat potential. Really now, only pregnant women have potential people inside of them. The true

MAKE A LIST OF ALL THE THINGS YOU LIKE ABOUT BEING FAT. TAPE IT TO THE REFRIGERATOR.

you is whatever size you were born to be—fat or thin. We're all shaped differently. Cookie cutters should only be used on dough, not on people!

* **ASSUMPTION:** Fat people are just hiding inside their fat—hiding from sex, from life, or perhaps from Jenny Craig (admittedly, a scary woman).

NEW VERSION: If you don't think fat is bad, you might assume that fat people are actually reaching out with their fat, to embrace life, not avoid it. You might realize that a fat person's body offers more luscious surface area, the better to enjoy tactile pleasures. In fact, if we saw fat people as normal, then we might assume that it's the *thin* people who are hiding, shrinking away from human interactions in their smaller bodies.

* **ASSUMPTION:** Fat people eat all the time.

NEW VERSION: Thin people eat all the time, too. (It's a really great survival skill.) In fact, studies show that fat people eat the same stuff that thin people do, from burgers to broccoli. One group of researchers tracked six thousand people, but could find no correlation between what they weighed and how much they ate. In our diet-crazy culture, when a fat person eats a bite of food, everyone notices.

* **ASSUMPTION:** Fat people aren't all that smart.

NEW VERSION: Um, no, actually, it's the people who believe in stereotypes who aren't thinking very much—and certainly aren't thinking for themselves!

* **ASSUMPTION:** Fat people are out of control.

NEW VERSION: Actually, I think we've been very restrained so far. If we *were* out of control, every time someone made some nasty comment about weight, we'd just sit on them until they apologized. If we got really good and out of control, we'd boycott the diet industry and show them who's boss. We'd run amok with chain saws, whacking out the armrests in movie theaters and commercial airliners. We'd stage sit-ins at New York fashion shows, in state legislatures, on beaches. Truly out-of-control fat people would refuse to apologize for their size. We'd act like we are all that and a bag of chips—and rightfully so. Fat people out of control? I can't wait!

* **ASSUMPTION:** All of the above, and then some: Fat people are smelly, stupid, lazy, gluttonous, sexless freaks.

NEW VERSION: These are the same slurs that have been applied to every stigmatized group, from people of color to the disabled. In the psychology of oppression, if you can belittle someone and deny their humanity, then it's okay to be hateful and prejudicial to them. These names are nothing new, and they say more about the person who invokes them than they ever could say about the people they claim to describe.

GAB CAFÉ
SUCCESS STORY #1: THE NEWLYWEDS

*I*N A COZY CORNER OF THE INTERNET, YOU *might stumble across the FAT!SO? Web site, www.fatso.com. Tap once on the door marked Hank's Gab Café, mumble the secret password, and you'll enter a wonderful place full of comfy chairs and hot and cold running lattés. Dozens of flabulous fat folk hang out there, day and night. Incredible stories unfold there all the time. This is one of them.*

Not long after Hank's Gab Café opened, Lori Shuler stopped by. It was her first time on the Internet, and she was checking out fat-positive Web sites. Something about Hank's just felt right to her. The gab was friendly and accepting. So Lori decided to post this message:

Any gentlemen still out there? If you qualify as a gentleman, I would love to hear from you via e-mail. I'm a super-sized lady, blonde hair, hazel eyes. Very down-to-earth and far from perfect, but I have a lot to offer someone who gives me the respect I deserve! I love this place!

That same day, a computer network engineer named James Fogg saw her message. "The day I sat down to answer personals ads, I had intended to answer quite a few, figuring that would increase my odds of finding someone. But I just felt really, really good about Lori's ad, so I didn't answer any more," James recalls. Lori's self-esteem impressed him. Plus, she sounded like just his type.

Lori got lots of replies to her message, but once she read the e-mail from James, he was the only person she could think about. James and Lori corresponded daily by e-mail and then by telephone. "The first time we talked, we just chatted and laughed for hours," Lori remembers.

They discovered they had lots in common. Lori lived in a small town in Pennsylvania, in the house where she grew up. James was living in Boston, not far from the small town where he

NONFAT MILK IS OKAY, THOUGH. I LIKE NONFAT MILK.

spent his youth, but he wasn't really a city person. James had spent years working with computers. Lori was just discovering that she loved Web-site design.

"I very much adored her from our e-mails and all the many hours every evening on the phone. I was deeply in love with her before she ever sent me her photo," James confesses. One night, Lori was telling James that she planned to make lasagna for dinner, and he said, "You know, I'm only marrying you for your lasagna."

Lori said, "Marry?"

He said, "Marry." Lori says that's when she knew for sure. She thought, "I just love this man!" She agreed that he should come for a visit.

"Waiting for him to make that six-hour drive down that first time was the longest day of my life," Lori recalls. "I had been through some rough times and a bad relationship before I met James. All of that made me realize that I really liked myself. Even if I was alone in life, it wouldn't be a bad thing, because I'm pretty good company. At the same time, I was a nervous wreck. I couldn't stand the thought of him showing up and saying, 'You're big, but I didn't know you were *that* big.'"

She needn't have worried. After their first meeting, James made the long drive every weekend,

through all sorts of weather, for nearly a year, until he could arrange to move to Pennsylvania.

"There was something that led us both to Hank's Gab Café," Lori says. "It was just so strange, we both had the feeling that we just had to do this, and it felt so right."

The next thing folks in Hank's Gab Café knew, Lori posted this message (less than three months after her first visit):

Thanks for giving me a place to come and feel welcome and appreciated. And extra thanks for letting me post some gab that ultimately allowed me to meet the most wonderful man on earth. He answered my post, and we decided to do the e-mail thing, which quickly turned into us both realizing that we were falling in love. I have found the true love that I have waited 36 years for.

I had decided that I would remain alone before I would keep company with anyone who didn't respect me. I was very comfortable with that decision, and it allowed me to be open and honest, and to give my love completely to a man who understands me and appreciates me exactly the way I am. What a wonderful feeling . . . all the crap in life that came before this was all worth it. It has allowed me to realize just how special the love is that I have found with my James. Thank you from the bottom of my heart for the chance to gab!

Lori and James were married September 27, 1997, exactly one year and five months after Lori's first message appeared in Hank's Gab Café.

XXX OOO
XXXX OOO

THE WASH & CHOP™ WAY

WELL, THIS WOULDN'T BE A BOOK FOR FAT people if it didn't contain some food advice. After all, I want to boost sales as much as any other author. Now, I *could* just point to the government's recommended food pyramid and say, "Eat that." But that wouldn't be any fun. I would be treating you like adults, with minds of your own, people who are able to decide for yourselves what's best for you, and then take the consequences, good or bad, based on those decisions. Respecting the reader's intelligence is surely the last thing that should *ever* happen in a book for fat people.

So here's my obligatory expert advice on how you should eat. If you don't follow this advice, your children will grow hunchbacks, your breath will smell, and you won't ever get laid again. (So much for the formulaic threat portion of my expert advice. Boy, does it sell books.)

Now, I'll proceed to restate stuff you already knew, using my own catchy language to make it sound like I'm revealing some earth-shattering new discovery.

First, get your grains. Then, chow down on as many veggies and fruits as you can stand. If you have any room left, go ahead and eat some meats and sweets. A little won't hurt ya! (Notice: I've simply restated the government's food pyramid, for those of you who found its little pictures and funny shape too confusing.)

But hey, I know that's a lot of rules to remember. I'll boil it all down to a simple slogan for you to follow mindlessly. (You've gotta have a catchphrase if you're going to write a best-seller.) Are you ready? Here it is: Wash & Chop™. That's it. You don't need to worry your little head with actual nutritional principles. Just remember to Wash & Chop™ once a day. There are no numbers to remember, no fat grams to count. Simply make sure that one meal you eat each day is stuff that you have to Wash & Chop™: bell

DON'T WAIT FOR SOMEONE TO ASK YOU TO DANCE. DO THE ASKING YOURSELF!

peppers, carrots, zucchini, apples, kiwis, all your fruits and vegetables. (Heck, make some ratatouille once in a while.) Of course, you should supplement the Wash & Chop™ foods with some Boil foods: pasta, brown rice, polenta, etc. But I don't want to make this too complicated!

Just remember, you can't Wash & Chop™ potato chips or donuts or ice cream or french fries, or anything that comes out of a drive-thru window, for that matter. You can still eat these foods, of course. They're food, after all! Simply supplement them once each day with items from the Wash & Chop™ category.

Now it's time for the ridiculous sacrifice portion of my food advice. For the Wash & Chop™ Way to work, you must never *ever* eat marzipan, ever again. Also, the health benefits of the Wash & Chop™ Way will be greatly enhanced if you dye your hair hot pink. Don't ask me why. Just take my word for it! Just Wash & Chop™! No marzipan! Dye your hair hot pink! And you're set for life.

K IS FOR KRIMINAL

"I have whipped people in order to help them and because they say they want to be whipped. It was strange and I admit it."

—Walter Kempner, inventor of the rice diet and director of Duke University's lucrative weight-loss center.

DIET DOUBLESPEAK

DOUBLESPEAK IS THE PROCESS OF TWISTING a word's meaning into its own opposite, while leaving the word itself intact. You don't notice the change, but whenever such a word is uttered, you find yourself jumping left instead of right (a really useful tool for getting people to go places they would normally avoid).

Some of the best-camouflaged doublespeak is diet doublespeak—the words we use to describe food and eating. For example, one hears the comment, "You need to take control." This actually means, "Relinquish all control of your food choices (what you eat, when you eat, and how much you eat) to us when you buy this diet plan for $29.95." (Or $295, or $2,950, or more.)

If a diet product claims to be filling or satisfying, you can pretty much count on being constantly hungry. "No deprivation" means "We've hired people to tell you those rumblings in your stomach are just gas." And, "Low fees! (not including the cost of food)" means you'll be paying $5 for a half cup of frozen mashed potatoes.

DON'T WAIT TO GET ASKED OUT ON DATES, EITHER! YOU'VE GOT A PHONE, TOO.

Thanks to diet doublespeak "the real you" doesn't look much like you at all. Your "after" photo is actually just the photo taken *before* your body regains its natural shape.

Perhaps the best example of diet double-speak is the word *healthy*—the single most dangerous word in our language today. In the United States, many people consider a 1,200-calorie-a-day diet healthy. In Ethiopia, the World Health Organization considers that starvation. Redux and Fen/Phen (aka Public Health Disaster #1 and #2) were supposed to make people healthy. Some millionaire surgeons with slick sales pitches claim that implanting a big rubber band to squeeze your stomach, or even stapling it, is healthy. (I think they have a weird thing for office products.) Living on bananas

---

The earth gains 40,000 TONS EACH YEAR from the space dust it picks up.

---

and crackers for weeks, sticking a finger down your throat, and hoping one day to weigh ninety-eight pounds is not healthy, either. How much more do we have to endure in the name of so-called health?

HOW TO TELL WHEN YOU'RE ON A DIET

* If you weigh yourself as often as you brush your teeth, you're on a diet.
* If you plan your social life around what you can or cannot eat, you're on a diet.
* If you're comforted by the thought that you can eat all the mushrooms you want, you're on a diet.
* If you've ever referred to a packet of gritty powder dissolved in water as a "shake," you're on a diet.
* If you've ever referred to a gritty drink in a can as a meal, you're on a diet.
* If you've ever said, "This isn't a diet, it's a lifestyle change!" you're on a diet.
* If you're trying to lose weight, then you're on a diet.
* If you've ever gained back more weight than you lost, you were on a diet.
* If you've ever said, "This time I'll keep the weight off," you're about to do it again.

WHEN YOU ENCOUNTER DIET ADS ON TV, POINT YOUR HAND AT 'EM LIKE A GUN, TAKE AIM, AND SHOOT THEM DOWN.
(GET CREATIVE WITH THE SOUND EFFECTS.)

* If you have to count anything you put in your mouth, you're on a diet.

* If you count the number of times you chew your food, you're on a very weird diet indeed.

* If you devote more space in your diary to what you eat each day than to what you did that day, you're on a really sick diet.

* If you think you can get "control" of your life by controlling what you eat, you're on a rather silly diet. (What you *really* need to reduce is your intake of pop psychology.)

* If all you talk about with coworkers over lunch is whether you're being "good" or "bad" by eating something, then you're on an embarrassing, adolescent kind of diet.

* If you utter the words, "May I have the sauce on the side?" you might be on a diet. (Note: Restaurant chefs know that people actually eat *more* sauce when it is served on-the-side. One ounce of sauce looks like plenty on the plate, but it takes four ounces to fill the little side dish. Either way, diners usually eat all the sauce provided.)

* If you think of your current weight as a plateau, you're on a diet.

* If you think that eating less food makes you a better person, your diet has taken over your life. Stop it!

FIRST STRIKE

WHAT'S COLORFUL, POWERFUL, HEAVY, and unashamed of plainly stating its weight? A bowling ball!

I came across a bowling ball at a garage sale not long ago. Its surface was swirly fuchsia and orange and yellow and it weighed ten pounds. I had to have it. I lugged it home and positioned it in a place of honor, resting on a little carved black-lacquer platform. Only then did I realize what a striking symbol of fat pride the bowling ball is. Bowling balls are beautiful, forceful, and open about their weight. They get to knock down the pinheads that get in their way. They have attitude to spare. (Plus, they get to roam around

90

inside the mysterious innards of those ball-return machines. How cool!) So I say, "All hail the beautiful, bounding bowling ball and everything it stands for!"

THE CYRANO SYNDROME

F THE DIET INDUSTRY INSISTS ON INSULTING the intelligence of fat Americans with their ridiculous weight-loss schemes, the least they could do is make the diets a bit more entertaining. In the spirit of Cyrano de Bergerac, here are some fictional fad diets that could easily work just as well as anything the diet industry has to offer. *And* some of them rhyme!

FENG-SHUI THE WEIGHT AWAY: Furniture arrangement that's guaranteed to make pounds disappear. Learn the secrets of interior decor that kept the Chinese ancestors slim and trim.

THE MIRACLE LEACHES DIET: Did you know that blood is mostly just water weight? Simply apply high-quality, American-bred leaches daily, and rid yourself of that serum for good. Feel light as an angel without excess liquid sloshing around in your veins.

THE ALPHABET DIET: A twenty-six-day diet organized alphabetically. Day one: eat foods that begin with the letter *A.* Day two: foods that start with *B,* and so on. Tough days like *Q* and *Z* come just when you've hit a plateau and need that extra discipline. Recite the alphabet out loud as you go up and down the grocery store aisles.

THE MUMMY DIET: Have a friend wrap you head-to-toe in Ace bandages and douse you liberally with mineral water (we like San Pellegrino). You might not lose any weight, but this regime will certainly take your mind off being fat for a while.

THE MASCARA DIET: Simply apply Max Factor's 2,000 Calorie Mascara to your lashes daily. (You know, the mascara where the TV ad says, "What's the one part of your body that can never be too fat?") Just think, mascara is so much cheaper and easier than buying groceries and then doing all that chewing, chewing, chewing—plus, no dirty dishes to wash! (Don't try this one at home, folks. Leave it to the professionals, models, that is.)

THE DIET BOOK DIET: For this diet, you'll need a home-sized paper shredder. It may seem expensive, but you'll find it's worth it. You'll also want to buy up a big stack of old diet books from thrift stores, used book stores, anywhere you can find them. Perhaps you even have some diet books lying around your own home. They're junk, of course, in their raw state—you know it, their previous owners knew it. But as roughage, diet books are invaluable. Simply pass the pages through the paper shredder and toss the resulting "pasta" with vegetables for dinner. Can you say *fiber?* (This diet works best for people who happen to have two stomachs.)

(Can you guess which of these crazy diets was actually on the market? Why, that would be the Mummy Diet! However, the name of this diet has been changed to protect the sleazy from further profits.)

OPPORTUNITY COST

AMERICANS SPEND ROUGHLY $40 BILLION A year on stuff we hope will make us thin. (That's *billion*, not *million*.) We buy diet sodas, diet foods, diet books, and diet videos. We choke down artificial sweeteners, appetite suppressants, and meal-replacement beverages. We go to commercial weight-loss centers again and

again. We risk liposuction, stomach stapling, and diet pills (despite their speedy withdrawal from the market).

Enough Americans are on diets right now to populate twenty-seven states, according to data compiled by Sondra Solovay. Yet the more we diet, the more weight we gain. In fact, you're more likely to survive cancer than you are to lose weight and keep it off. It would seem that we're wasting about $40 billion each year. That's a ton of money, and a ton of anguish. Here are some ways we could put that money to good use, instead. (What we could do with all the wasted hours and wasted effort is another story.)

With $40 billion, each year we could . . .

* Put one third of all graduating high school seniors in the United States through four years of college. That amounts to the entire 1998 high school graduating classes from California, New York, Texas, Ohio, and Iowa.

* Fund the government's entire 1998 budget for Veterans Affairs.

* Pay off the federal deficit—twice.

* Heat and serve a breakfast of two Pop-Tarts to every man, woman, and child in the United States—five days a week—for an entire year. (That's 160 billion tasty Pop-Tarts in 20 billion boxes.)

TALK WITH CHILDREN ABOUT FAT PRIDE. DON'T BE SHY. THEY DESPERATELY NEED TO HEAR IT.

* Build 2.5 Habitat for Humanity homes for each of the 2.5 million homeless people in the U.S.
* Donate four times more money to charities than the combined charitable donations from all U.S. corporations.

Typhoon-class subs in the world.)
* Run ninety-seven women's universities.
* Fund the National Endowment for the Arts for 250 years.

Or we could . . .

Each second, the earth is hit by 4.5 POUNDS OF SUNLIGHT, or 70,000 TONS of sunlight PER YEAR.

---

* Provide six times more federally funded day care to help working parents.
* Provide six times more money for the Environmental Protection Agency.
* Allocate eight times more federal funding for AIDS research, prevention, and treatment.
* Provide nine times as many free school lunches to hungry children.
* Run the entire federal government for nine whole days.
* Acquire thirteen small Fortune 500 companies.
* Buy twenty B-2 Stealth bombers, one less than the U.S. government has.
* Increase Medicaid services nationwide by nearly 40 percent.
* Purchase forty Soviet-made Typhoon submarines, each equipped with twenty nuclear-tipped ICBMs. (Not really. There are only six

* Start an airline with 400 new 747 jet airplanes. (And install comfy seats!)
* Install 840 new Power Macintosh computers in every single public high school in the United States.
* Equip our own private air force with more than 1,300 F16-C fighter jets, the U.S. Navy's newest attack craft.
* Operate 4,000 women's health clinics.
* Create 66,000 battered women's shelters.
* Drive three million new, four-door cars from Saturn. (That's a new car for everyone in the Atlanta, Georgia, metropolitan area.)
* Buy 285 million pairs of Nike Air Jordan athletic shoes. That's enough to give a pair of Air Jordans to every single person in America (with 17 million pairs left over).
* Take everyone on Earth out to see a movie.

LEARN A NEW RECIPE THAT HAS BROCCOLI AS A MAIN INGREDIENT. YOUR BODY LOVES THE STUFF.

YEAH, RIGHT!

OLE'S ORIGINAL COMEBACK

A kid recently shouted at me, "You big thermos bottle." Was he referring to my size? My brown winter coat? Or could he tell that I'm a person filled with warmth and good things?

—OLE JOERGEN MALM

MICHELLE'S MARVELOUS COMEBACK

I once worked in a large department store, in the women's sizes. Often we would have a size 6 person who did not realize the difference between "women" as a clothing size and women as a gender, and she would end up in my area by mistake. I would explain the difference pleasantly and direct them to the area they needed. But sometimes, if the person was rude, I would reply, "Yes, this is the women's department, and when your brain and your body finally develop into womanhood I am sure I will be able to help you." Not very useful for most people, but it helped me get through the day. Believe it or not, I was not fired from that job.

—MICHELLE HAEGLE

JOHANNE'S JUST COMEBACK

I've been known to get bitchy at men who tell me, "You'd be gorgeous if you lost some of that weight." I just say, "Uh huh. You may say you don't like it in the streets, but you know you love it in the sheets. . . . I don't buy it. If you're not man enough to admit you like me as I am, then what makes you think you're gonna be man enough for me?"

Another classic situation: Someone hands me a "Lose weight now, ask me how!" flier. I respond, "Eat shit and die, ask me why!"

—JOHANNE BLANK

PATIA'S TOP-TEN LIST OF COMEBACKS

1. In response to "No Fat Chicks" bumper stickers: "No Stupid Dudes."
2. In response to drive-by harassment: a big smile and wave.
3. In response to a query about the state of my reproductive system: Nope, I'm not pregnant, I'm just fat (with a confident smile).
4. In response to little kids who comment on my weight or size: A cheerful, "Yup, I sure am fat. Isn't it great?"
5. In response to ignorant comments by teens or grown-ups: Grow a brain.
6. In response to people announcing the new diet they're on: "Oh, are you trying to gain weight?"
7. In response to, "You have such a beautiful face.": "Yeah, and a fabulous body, too. I'm so lucky."
8. In response to "Have you lost weight?": "I hope not!" Or, "Why? Do I look bad?" Or, "Oh, no, I'd better go order a milkshake!"
9. In response to people who say fat is not sexy: "That's funny. Fat women have a higher sex drive and more orgasms than thin women. What's not sexy about that?"
10. In response to most any rude comment: "And I should care because . . . ?"

And here's my favorite recent comeback moment: It happened when a Victoria's Secret saleswoman asked me if I'd found everything I was looking for, and I said, "Yeah, everything except my size."

—PATIA STEPHENS

KATHY'S QUICK COMEBACK

An all-purpose favorite: Who died and made you Richard Simmons?

—KATHY BARRON

PANDA'S REM-STATE COMEBACK

I had this crazy dream once involving comebacks to people's attitudes about fat. In the dream, I get on an elevator that seems to be in my place of work. A female co-worker gets on with me, all smiley and bubbly. She says, "I just found this brand new diet! It's great!"

"Wait," I said, "I'll bet mine is even better. You can eat anything you want to any time you want to—no restrictions." I stand there and smile. She stands there and waits. The elevator stops and I get off.

—CLAUDIA STRONG

EAT LIKE A BIRD

F YOU REALLY *DID* EAT LIKE A BIRD, YOU WOULD consume ten times your weight in food every day. You'd have to eat a big breakfast, just to regain the weight you lost during the night.

And if you were a hummingbird, skipping breakfast could send you into a deadly coma. If you really *did* eat like a horse, you'd have to consume fifteen pounds of hay every day, with a couple quarts of oats thrown in for balance. And you'd wash down this small mountain of roughage with a big trough of water.

L IS FOR LUSCIOUS

"Everything you see I owe to spaghetti."
—Sophia Loren, actress

"Food is an important part of a balanced diet."
—Fran Lebowitz, humorist

GENETIC CURSES

by Emily Ivie

OU'D PROBABLY HATE ME BECAUSE I'M THIN. I'm thin because my Mom is a freakin' stick. She had eleven children and is still under 110 pounds. I hate being thin. I hate being called fat by anorexic thin people who think that if you don't wear a shirt three sizes too small you must have something to hide. And I hate it when my sisters all say, "You're losing weight!" like it's a compliment. I hate it that my favorite sister-in-law got her stomach stapled because Fen/Phen wouldn't cut it and she had to sit around at all the family gatherings listening to the aforementioned sisters, who hardly clear 110 pounds themselves, talk about dieting and losing weight 100 percent of the time.

I hate it that my best friend, who's "overweight" (whatever *that* means), got taken to an Amway meeting on a date with a guy she had a crush on. (All the while, *he* loved her anorexic friend.) I hate it that my significant other has been conditioned by his mother to think I'm going to dump him if he doesn't lose weight. I hate the way my family looks at him and thinks he's a lazy bum and a slob, as if weight implies that. I hate the way people say that so-called

SAVE ON WINTER FUEL BILLS—BURN YOUR OLD DIET BOOKS IN THE FIREPLACE. WHAT A CHEERY GLOW!

overweight people are unhealthy, but they never mention the health risks of being underweight. I hate it that in a recent poll, little six-year-olds would rather lose an arm than be fat. And I hate it that whenever I say anything, no one listens because I'm thin and, "It doesn't matter to me."

But I have one hope: Once body fat drops below a certain percentage, the body shuts down its reproductive organs. If society keeps on this merry track, maybe Darwinism will kick in and save us all!

NOTES FROM A YOUNG ZINE EDITOR

WAS SO PLEASED WITH THE FIRST ISSUE OF *FAT!SO?* that I wanted to tell the whole fat world about it. I pondered the problem: How could I reach fat people? Where do they hang out?

Of course! Weight Watchers! I called their New York office. They told me that *Weight Watchers* magazine reaches 1,035,322 people who think about fat all the time. I was overjoyed. *Weight Watchers* magazine readers would surely want to know about *FAT!SO?*. I talked with the magazine's advertising representative. She seemed to think Weight Watchers might not want to sell me an ad in their magazine. But she told me to send her a copy of my proposed ad, and she'd see what she could do. I designed a very simple *FAT!SO?* ad. It just had the name, subscription information, and the tag line. You know, the *FAT!SO?* slogan: "for people who don't apologize for their size!"

I was pretty excited to buy a big-time ad with a big-time price tag. The cheapest ad in *Weight Watchers* magazine (1/12 of a page, or about two square inches) would cost $1,733. Whew. But if just one tenth of one percent of their one million readers subscribed to *FAT!SO?*, not only would I sign up a thousand new readers, I could make 12,000 bucks. Enough to boost *FAT!SO?* into its own big time.

Then I got the call from the Weight Watchers ad rep. "Sorry," she said. "They decided not to accept your ad." Incredulous, I asked why, what was wrong with my money? "They found the *FAT!SO?* ad offensive," she finally admitted.

Well, here are some things that I find offensive about Weight Watchers. Weight Watchers funds medical researchers who, oddly enough, often tell fat people to lose weight or else. Weight Watchers and Jenny Craig are corporate sponsors of former surgeon general C. Everett Koop's "new" war on fat. Weight Watchers counts each person who loses and regains the same twenty pounds five different times on their program as five "successes." That's not really success, but it sure is profitable.

COTTAGE CHEESE CUISINE

SINCE I'VE NEVER SUFFERED THROUGH A DIET, I actually enjoy a lot of traditional diet foods. Cottage cheese, for example. I love to eat it as a snack or a meal. Here are a couple of my favorite cottage cheese recipes:

* **COTTAGE CHEESE AND PEAS CURRY:** Sauté a chopped onion in some curry paste. Add a carton of frozen peas and a little water. Simmer until the peas are warmed through. Remove the pan from the heat and add a small container of cottage cheese. Stir thor-

oughly. The cottage cheese will melt to a gooey goodness. Serve over brown rice. (I made this dish up myself, using things they sell at my corner store.)

* **COTTAGE CHEESE VEGGIE DIP:** Chop some tomatoes, carrots, and bell pepper in small bits. Add these veggies and a dollop of mayonnaise to a regular container of cottage cheese. Mix it all up together. For extra numminess, mash up a ripe avocado and mix it in, too. Mmmmm. Scoop up this dip on sturdy tortilla chips for a crunchy, creamy taste treat. (This one is a Mom classic, and a great snack to serve while watching WNBA games with the gals.)

* **COTTAGE CHEESE SURPRISE:** Put some cottage cheese on a plate. Top it with spaghetti sauce from a jar. Microwave very briefly, probably thirty seconds or less. Experiment with your microwave to find the exact duration of cooking time that turns this dish into a remarkable faux pasta. (The brilliant Sondra Solovay taught me how to make this.)

Sadly, a fat woman cannot live on cottage cheese alone. I also get cravings for broccoli. Broccoli is another one of those notorious diet foods that I never learned to hate because I never took it medicinally. I especially love broccoli the way my mother makes it, steamed and then swirled with a little margarine. When I cook broccoli, though, it's usually in stir-fry, where it develops that dark green color and ultra-veggie flavor. I also toss blanched broccoli in salads, use it leftover in quick scrambled eggs, and smush it into buttery baked potatoes. If I don't eat broccoli at least once a week, I get the cruciform jitters. I wish our language had words for all the ecstatic flavor nuances of broccoli: the raw-potato tang of uncooked broccoli, the sweet balance of broccoli that is not quite cooked and not quite raw, the rich aroma of broccoli fresh from its steamy sauna. Mm, mm, num! Don't get me started on boneless skinless chicken breasts, now! Suffice it to say, traditional diet foods taste great, as long as you're not on a diet.

FOODS I REALLY DON'T LIKE (PLEASE, TAKE MINE, I DON'T WANT ANY!)

❊ **CHEESECAKE**
Thick, mealy, sticky, horrible stuff. Give me a nice chocolate mousse any day.

❊ **BIRTHDAY CAKE WITH ICE CREAM**
Separately, they're delicious, but please, not both on the same plate. Icing and melted ice cream is just not a good combo. And how am I supposed to eat it with a plastic fork?

❊ **MILK CHOCOLATE**
Really, why bother when you can have the dark stuff instead?

❊ **CARAMEL**
I'm just not fond of any food that adheres to my teeth.

M IS FOR MEAN

"If American men are obsessed with money, American women are obsessed with weight. The men talk of gain, the women talk of loss, and I do not know which talk is the more boring."

—Marya Mannes, feature editor at *Vogue* and *Glamour* during the thirties and forties, later a TV commentator and nationally syndicated columnist.

Student: "What's the meanest thing said to you when you were a student at the prestigious Parsons School of Design?"

Isaac Mizrahi: "What's the meanest thing anyone could ever say to you? You're fat."

—Isaac Mizrahi, fashion designer, during an appearance at San Francisco's Academy of Art College.

EAT WHEN YOU'RE HUNGRY. NEVER APOLOGIZE FOR IT.

GAB CAFÉ SUCCESS STORY #2: THE ANGRY YOUNG WOMAN

WHEN TWENTY-THREE-YEAR-OLD COLLEEN Hegedus first visited Hank's Gab Café on the *FAT!SO?* Web site (www.fatso.com), she was popping up to twelve Ex-Lax a day and living on Saltines and watermelon to keep her weight down to 115 pounds. We didn't know anything about that at the time. All we knew was that someone was attacking us and everything *FAT!SO?* stands for.

In her first message, Colleen wrote:

I've been sitting here reading as people praise themselves for being fat. Hello! Has anyone here heard of heart disease, diabetes, and all the other horrible things that happen to fat people? I was once a "fatso" but thanks to some common sense and a lot of willpower I am no longer part of the "fatso" group. Aren't you people embarrassed every time you go into a store only to find that there aren't any clothes that fit you? Or when you have trouble getting out of a chair because your butt is stuck to the sides? Aren't you ashamed to go to the beach in a bathing suit? Wake up everyone. Fat is not beautiful. It is pathetic.

From this beginning, we never could have predicted that Colleen would become a dear friend, or that the Café would be a major support in her battle with eating disorders. Colleen remembers:

I had started to realize I had a problem. One night, I was searching the Internet for Web sites about bulimia, when I came across FAT!SO?. The name alone piqued my interest, and then the first thing I see is a bunch of butts! It just boggled my mind. I hated myself being fat. So how on earth could anyone love themselves? I was just so enraged. I thought, "What's the matter with you people?"

At first, Gabsters just got angry and argued with Colleen. We tried to explain how fat people can indeed be healthy and happy. We questioned her fat-hating attitudes. Colleen kept coming back to argue with us. It seemed like neither side was going to budge. Then, after nearly a week of hot debate, we got the first clue. Colleen mentioned that she hated not being able to find a pretty prom dress when she was a size 16. An especially wise Gabster named Sydney respond-

DON'T LET ANYONE TELL YOU HOW TO EAT. FOLLOW YOUR OWN APPETITE. BUT I STILL RECOMMEND BROCCOLI.

ed, "I'm beginning to wonder if maybe Colleen is just a confused teenager who needs our loving support and education more than our anger. Colleen, honey . . . it doesn't matter if your prom dress is a size 16 or a size 6. Everything is going to work out fine for you. Don't fret."

At that point, Colleen decided to explain why it was so impossible for her to believe in happy fat people. Colleen wrote:

I grew up in a family where if you were even ten pounds overweight, you were subhuman. My mother was so embarrassed that her nine-year-old little girl was chubby. Actually, I think she just plain called me FAT. I was always compared to my thin, blonde, pretty sister. I was always made to feel that if you are fat, you are nothing. And there isn't a single one of you who can't tell me that at one point or other you haven't felt the same way! Since I was sixteen years old I have suffered from bulimia at different times. Trying to find a prom dress that would somewhat flatter me, pleasing my boyfriend who was upset by my weight, pleasing my family who constantly ridiculed me for being fat ... all these things were huge factors. One day, about a year and a half ago, I decided to eat "healthy." I lost a lot of weight and for the first time in my

entire life people told me how great I looked. Who wouldn't feel good about that? And now I find myself battling not only bulimia but anorexia as well. I weigh about 112 pounds, and people still say I look great, but there's always that fear that I'm going to get fat again and people will stop praising me. You all are happy with yourselves. That's fine. I'm not. I'll probably be happy when I weigh ninety-five pounds. I was brought up in a world where fat is gross. I'm not asking you to feel sorry for me. I'm just trying to show a little perspective on why I think the way I do.

At that point, everyone in the Gab Café did a 180-degree turn. Our anger disappeared and the argument ended. Gabsters offered Colleen their care and support. Everyone there could certainly understand self-hatred. I posted phone numbers for eating disorder hotlines, and those who had survived their own battles with food reassured Colleen that it was a fight she could win. During the next week, we got to know more about her and what she'd been through. After all the anger, it was wonderful to see all her good qualities.

Our body-positive attitudes began to rub off a little on Colleen, too. Two weeks after her first visit to the Café, she wrote:

NOURISH YOUR BODY WELL, BECAUSE YOU'RE WORTH IT.

I bought the prettiest little mint green linen suit this weekend and couldn't wait to put it on for work. When I looked into the mirror, instead of frowning and wondering if I looked fat ... I smiled! Everyone at work told me I looked great, and I felt great, too. Somehow, I felt that I was pretty as I am now, not twenty pounds thinner. I actually smiled in the mir-

one hour with someone who's specially trained to help you?" I offered her a deal. If she would go to one appointment with an eating disorder specialist, I'd get her the best referral I could.

Colleen wrote:

I spent tonight really thinking about things and have decided that I can't live this way. I can't go through life with a box of Ex-Lax in my

---

At the height of the civil rights movement in the 1960s, there were about 22 MILLION AFRICAN AMERICANS. When Harvey Milk was elected as a supervisor in San Francisco in the 1970s, 150,000 GAYS AND LESBIANS were living in the city. In the 1980s, when the Americans with Disabilities Act was passed by Congress, there were 49 MILLION DISABLED PEOPLE in the United States. In the 1990s, there are now 97 MILLION FAT AMERICANS.

---

ror for the first time in months! Thank you!!!

We were thrilled for Colleen, but we still encouraged her to get some help from a professional. She worried that a therapist would force her to eat and get fat again. We assured her that no one could make her do anything she didn't want to do. Then I said, "Hey, Colleen, which do you think is tougher? Winning over a whole bunch of angry fat activists, or spending

purse. Learning to accept myself as is will take a long time, but I'm trying. Coming to the Café was probably the best thing I could have done. You guys are making me see that I do have a problem and that I'm a whole person despite my body appearance. Thank you all so much. I love you guys!

Three weeks after her first visit to the Gab Café, Colleen took me up on my offer and made her first

EXERCISE, BECAUSE YOU'RE WORTH IT.

appointment with an eating disorder specialist.

We didn't hear as much from Colleen for a little while. She spent a month doing intensive therapy, traveled for a while, and started spending time with a new boyfriend, one who wasn't obsessed with her weight. When she checked back in again at the Café, she had been purge-free for five months. Colleen is a smart, determined woman. When she says that she's going to beat her eating disorder, I believe her. I'm both honored and grateful that Hank's Gab Café could offer her some support on the way.

Colleen says now:

I owe so much of my happiness now to the Café. When I was in therapy, no one said, "You're okay how you are. It's okay to be Colleen. You don't have to be a perfect size 6. It's okay to be a perfect size 16." There's no warmth. They just asked questions: Why? Why? Why? It was depressing. In the Café, no one cares what you look like. They don't care if I gain twenty pounds or lose twenty pounds. They care about me. They're always sending virtual hugs. And when I have a setback, they don't judge me. They just say, "Hey, you've had a stumble. We love you! Get back up and get going." When people ask me how I'm dealing with my eating disorder, I'm not ashamed to say, "I went to a Web site with a bunch of fat people." Four or five months ago, I saw myself as huge and unloveable. There are still days when I wake up and feel that way. But those days are fewer than the days when I'm happy with how I am. And I owe it all to the Café. I finally understood that you guys weren't saying, "I'm happy to be fat." You were saying, "I'm happy to be me." And that's the greatest thing, to be able to get up in the morning and say, "I like myself how I am, and if you don't like it, deal."

WHY NOT JUST NEEDLEPOINT?

MY FRIEND CHARLES RAN INTO ME ONE DAY at the corner cafe in our neighborhood. He was all excited. I asked why.

"I'm going to start this great new, eight-week plan to optimize my health," Charles said.

"I didn't know you weren't feeling good," I said.

"Oh, I feel fine, but I *could* feel better," Charles said, eyes widening for emphasis.

"Did you buy some kind of diet book?" I asked. Charles knows that I think diet books are not

FIND A PHYSICAL ACTIVITY THAT YOU ENJOY AND THAT FEELS GOOD.

only a waste of time and money, but an exercise in self-hatred.

"Of course not! This is a book about getting as healthy as you can. I saw this guy on PBS last night, and I actually watched two of his shows in a row, because he was smart and kinda funny. So today I went out and bought his book," Charles said, his excitement mounting.

"Charles, you never watch TV. And you're not usually taken in by a charismatic sales pitch. What's wrong?" I asked.

"Nothing's wrong. I just think that doing this eight-week program will be good for me. You see, the house is a mess right now, and I don't feel like cleaning. Mark and I haven't even been cooking or eating at home for the past week. We hardly spend any time together. I just need to do something," Charles explained.

"So what you really need to do is stop watching TV, talk to your boyfriend, do some dishes, and get back to your normal routine—*not* embark on some weird food plan," I said, doing my best impersonation of a nosy neighbor.

"Yeah, but I don't wanna do all that stuff. This program will be fun," Charles argued.

"Let me see this book," I said. I flipped to the book's index. It had several listings under diet, obesity, and weight loss. I flipped to one of the page references for weight loss. "Look here, Charles. This guy says that if you follow his program, you won't be fat. He's pushing a diet!"

"But that's not why I'm doing this," Charles protested. Admittedly, neither Charles nor his boyfriend Mark are fat, and neither of them is trying to lose weight. (In fact, Charles has a little starter belly that he's very proud of; and he dreams of gaining enough weight to wear pants with a thirty-two-inch waist.) They both go to the gym several times a week and cook tons of fresh vegetables and grains at home. It would be hard to imagine a healthier pair.

"So why did you plunk down $29.95 for this book, Charles? Aren't you just avoiding the stuff you really need to do? I mean really, if you want to take up a new hobby, why not just *needlepoint*? It'd certainly be more productive than going on this program. And when you get bored with needlepointing, at least you'll have handmade gifts to give all your friends!" I ranted.

Then I got to thinking about all the millions of people on diets—a fourth of the adults in the United States—and I thought about how needlepoint used to be just as popular, perhaps more popular, than dieting is now. In all those Masterpiece Theatre shows, the well-to-do women spend a lot of time stitching. In fact, for

EVERYONE NEEDS A HOBBY

✽ NEEDLEPOINT
NATIONAL NEEDLEWORK
ASSOCIATION
1100-H Brandywine Blvd.
P.O. Box 2188
Zanesville, Ohio 43702
(800) 889-8662

✽ WOODWORKING
(MY DAD'S A MEMBER.
HE LOVES IT.)
AMERICAN ASSOCIATION OF
WOODTURNERS
3200 Lexington Avenue
Shoreview, Minnesota
55126
Web site:
www.RTPnet.org/~aaw

✽ SWING DANCE
(IT'S HIP, DADDY-O.)
*Swing! the New Retro
Renaissance*
A 1998 book edited by V.
Vale and Marian Wallace.

Available from V/Search
20 Romolo, Suite B
San Francisco, CA 94133
(415) 362-1465
Web site:
www.vsearchmedia.com
E-mail:
research@sirius.com

U.S. SWING DANCE SERVER
A great Web site for swing
resources and links to
other dance sites.
http://simon.cs.cornell.edu
/Info/People/aswin/SwingD
ancing/swing_dancing.html

✽ ZINE PUBLISHING
(THIS IS ONE HOBBY
THAT CAN REALLY
CHANGE YOUR LIFE.)
FACTSHEET FIVE: THE
DEFINITIVE GUIDE TO THE
ZINE REVOLUTION
P.O. Box 170099
San Francisco CA 94117
Web site:
www.factsheet5.com

✽ BACKGAMMON
(MY PERSONAL FAVORITE)
*Flint Area
Backgammon News*
Carol Joy Cole, publisher
3719 Greenbrook Lane
Flint, Michigan 48507-1400
Web site: home-
page.interaccess.com/~ska
tz/flint.html
cjc@flint.org
(810) 232-9731

Chicago Point
Bill Davis, publisher
3940 W. Bryn Mawr Avenue
#504
Chicago, Illinois
60659-3155
Web site: home-
page.interaccess.com/~chi
point/
chipoint@interaccess.com
(773) 583-6464

centuries, women spent their days worrying over needlework of one sort or another. They based their self-esteem on the quality and intricacy of their delicate stitches; it said something about what kind of women they were. Nowadays, women (and increasingly men) spend their days worrying over the fine points of calories and fat grams. As if *that* says something about what kind of people we are.

I told Charles my new theory. He admitted that it sounded good, then said, "But I think I'll still try this program for a while." I smiled, because it really is a wonder that he puts up with my meddling.

A couple weeks later, I thought to ask Charles how optimal his health had gotten. At first he didn't know what I was talking about.

"Y'know, the eight-week thing?" I asked.

"Oh that! I never bothered with it. I realized it was just stuff I already know," he said. "Hey. See how big my belly's getting? Cool, huh?"

As this little story demonstrates, most people don't start a diet out of some grand desire to improve their health or even to decrease their weight. Most of us start diets because we're bored, and we're looking around for some kind of distraction—a distraction that makes us feel like we're Really Doing Something.

Maybe the kids have gone back to school, and you have a lot of extra time to obsess about your thighs. Maybe you just broke up with your boyfriend, and you want something to take your mind off it. Maybe your first job out of college doesn't really challenge you, and you're looking for something to ease that vague feeling of purposelessness. Maybe you're just watching TV one night, trying to relax, and some diet guru lectures you about all the stuff you should be doing instead of sitting and watching TV (ironic, huh?).

In the fifties, when people were bored and needed a distraction, they took up hobbies. I think the hobby is an underrated art form that deserves a revival. They are inexpensive, productive, fulfilling, and harmless. With a traditional hobby, you collect something or make something or practice some odd physical skill, like juggling. Ideally, a hobby is something you enjoy doing. It should, in some small way, make you a better person and give you something to show for your efforts, something that you'll enjoy sharing with other people.

Given these criteria, dieting is clearly a poor choice for a hobby. First, diets are expensive, unhealthy, unproductive (since you're likely to regain the weight), and not particularly fun. What's worse, when you're on a diet, you mis-

DON'T DO ANY KIND OF EXERCISE IF IT HURTS. NO PAIN . . . NO PAIN.

takenly assume that other people are as interested in fat grams as you are. You become a bore. It's not a pretty sight. Instead, why not try a real hobby? Something worth your while? Go hiking. Take pottery classes. Learn to play the ukelele. Join a reading group. Get a small needlepoint kit and see if you like it.

THE DANCE OF HAPPINESS

by Yalith Fonfa

AT AGE TWELVE, I WEIGHED 125 POUNDS. I thought I was fat. After all, my best friend only weighed 108 pounds. I hated my body. I tried everything that a twelve year old can do to lose weight. When I went to the doctor for a physical for school, she said, "Your weight is okay now—just watch what you eat. You shouldn't gain any more weight unless you grow a lot." I took that to mean, "You weigh what an adult who is taller than you should weigh." I told myself I was a little fat. I could lose weight. I did. Then puberty hit full on. My breasts and my hips got much bigger. I went up to 135 pounds. I got very depressed. I was then convinced that I was *really* fat.

On the night of my school's modern dance performance, I crashed emotionally. I crashed from dieting and self-deprivation and self-hatred. As soon as I walked off the stage, I burst into tears. I wouldn't talk to my friends. My dance teacher and I went into the theater department office. We talked for two hours and made my parents wait in the car. I don't remember exactly what was said. But somewhere in that conversation, I stopped hating my body. I finally started to realize that I was going to be fat. All the women in my family are fat. Since I was a little kid, I'd always weighed more than my friends. Then it dawned on me: "So what? Maybe I am fat. Why is that a bad thing?" From that day on, I have loved my body. After I stopped dieting and started being a healthy person, my weight went up to 150 pounds. My doctor had a talk with me about that. I pointed out to her that, overall, I am much healthier than I used to be. I have more energy, and most importantly, I spend my time thinking about important things, instead of how much I miss good food.

Now I am fourteen years old. I weigh 150 pounds. I love my body and for once in my life, I don't want to lose weight. I am happier now than I have ever been. It is because I love myself, inside and out.

107

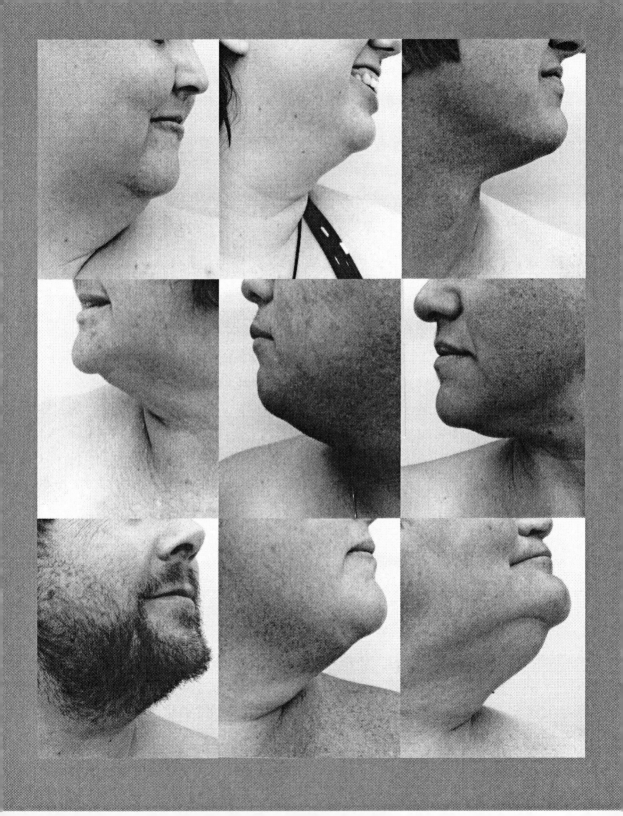

ANATOMY LESSON #3

THE
CHIN

IT AIN'T NECESSARILY SO

ERE'S PROOF THAT BEING FAT OR THIN IS no longer about appearance, or even about health, but has turned into a question of moral, nay religious, importance. A new breed of diet guru, the Christian diet guru, would have us believe that God cares what you weigh. There are evidently thousands of "Slim Down with Jesus" programs in churches these days. There's even something called *The Angels' Little Diet Book: Heavenly Hints to Help You Fight Fat!*

Before you start heeding the new commandment, "Thou shalt be thin," check out this comparison of quotes from Christian diet books with quotes from another good book:

WHAT THE DIET-VANGELISTS SAY	WHAT THE BIBLE SAYS
"The fat, sluggish Christian displays in his body the identifying marks of his real master—THE DEVIL!" writes C.S. Lovett, in his 1977 book, *Help, Lord ... the Devil Wants Me Fat!*	"The soul of the sluggard desireth, and *hath* nothing: but the soul of the diligent shall be made fat." (Proverbs 13:4)
"Is it any worse for the Lord to find you in bed with someone else's wife or husband? Or to have Him find you twenty to fifty pounds overweight?" Lovett also writes.	"And the Lord shall guide thee continually, and satisfy thy soul in drought and make fat thy bones ..." (Isaiah 58:11)
"As you settle down in bed, thank Him for the nice, new figure He is giving you," writes Lovett, who believes ten-day, water-only fasts and meditation are the way to a Godly weight.	"He that withholdeth corn, the people shall curse him ..." (Proverbs 11:26)
In 1967, Percy Cerutty wrote a book called, *Be Fit! Or Be Damned!*	"The liberal soul shall be made fat." (Proverbs 11:25)
"You won't do all you could for Christ [if you're] sleeping off the sugar blues." says the Honor God with Your Body Web site.	"He that is of a proud heart stirreth up strife: but he that putteth his trust in the Lord shall be made fat." (Proverbs 28:25)

17 FUN THINGS
TO DO WITH YOUR
BATHROOM SCALE
(THAT DON'T INVOLVE WEIGHING YOURSELF!)

MODERN-DAY INVENTIONS HAVE THE POWER to change our lives. Just try to imagine a world without the telephone, the atomic bomb, the bathroom scale.

Of course, telephones vastly improved communication, and the bomb vastly improved the whole destruction thing. Meanwhile, the bathroom scale made it possible for Americans to obsess about weight on a daily basis. What kind of an invention is that? Since bathroom scales became popular in the 1920s, we've seen the rise of the diet industry, the creation of the height/weight chart, and the spread of an eating disorder epidemic. Although we can never get rid of phones or bombs, we *can* rid our lives of at least one invention that's caused untold human pain and suffering: the bathroom scale.

Of course, you could simply toss your bathroom scale in the trash can, but after all the damage it's done, it deserves a fate far worse than banishment. Here are some amusing and therapeutic suggestions for doing away with your bathroom scale:

* Paint a bull's-eye on it and use it as a target for suction-cup darts.
* Use it as an anchor for your dinghy.
* Marbleize your bathroom scale, à la Martha Stewart. Voilà, a tasteful bookend.
* Turn the bathroom scale into a device for telling the future.

STEP 1: Pop out the little window.

STEP 2: Cut delightful words and pictures out of magazines.

STEP 3: Glue them all over the numbers on the scale.

STEP 4: Replace the little window.

STEP 5: Step on the scale each morning to see what kind of day you're going to have. It's better than the Magic Eight Ball. Consult your souped-up scale about thorny relationship problems. Let your new bathroom scale completely determine what your day will be like, just like in the old days.

* Encase your bathroom scale in shag carpeting and give your cats a new scratching post.

* Place it under potted plants to avoid getting nasty water rings on the windowsill, tabletop, or wooden floors.

* Toss your bathroom scale through a big, plate-glass window at your local diet store. (Tie a friendly, fat-positive note around it first with twine.)

* Donate it to your local right-wing militia group for target practice.

* Tile the floor of your local art gallery with bathroom scales and call it an installation. (Watch people's reactions as they sip chardonnay from little plastic cups and walk around on the "art.")

* Put your bathroom scale in a 200-degree oven for fifteen minutes on frosty winter mornings (this works best with all-metal models). Place it on the driver's seat while you scrape the windows of your car. By the time you're ready to go, your seat will be nice and toasty. (Be sure to remove the scale before you get in the car.)

* Once the winter's over, set your bathroom scale in the driveway and drive back and forth over it with your car. Take the remains to the dump and recycle the metal.

* Remove the innards from your bathroom scale, scrawl a fat-positive slogan on it, add some postage, and mail it to the diet guru of your choice.

* Use it to prop up a wobbly coffee table.

* Paint bathroom scales pretty colors and use them in your garden as stepping-stones.

* Reprogram the voice chip inside a talking bathroom scale to recite body-positive statements.

* Invite some kids to jump up and down on it. Time them, and see how long it takes to break the thing.

* Get your friends together on May 6, International No-Diet Day, and crush your bathroom scales with sledgehammers. Do it somewhere in public. Invite your local TV news cameras. It'll be smashing.

N IS FOR No

Pinky & the Brain is a TV cartoon about two lab mice. In one episode, they decide they're going to move the earth, and Brain realizes it's too heavy.

Brain: "How are we going to get the earth to lose weight?"

Pinky: "I know! We can get every-one to go on a diet!"

Brain: "Diets don't work."

Pinky: "Not even if you call them 'A Whole New Way of Eating'?"

Brain: "No."

—Pinky & the Brain

IT'S HEREDITARY

DIETING, LIKE SO MANY DYSFUNCTIONAL behaviors, is usually learned in the home. Perhaps it's more like a religion, and you can be raised a calorie counter, just like you can be raised Catholic.

In some houses, children grow up with parents who are always on diets. Little girls, especially, grow up believing that going hungry is part of becoming a woman. In their ambition for full personhood, they sometimes forget to eat at all. (Not every diet leads to an eating disorder, but everyone who has an eating disorder started by dieting.)

My parents were diet disbelievers. I've never gone on a diet, probably because my mother never taught me how. In her house, you eat three squares a day: cereal for breakfast, sandwich or soup for lunch, and a meat-and-two-veg meal for dinner, followed by dessert on occasion. There isn't much snacking. On the weekend, you get eggs and bacon for breakfast. (Man, those eggs are good.)

For me, not dieting also meant not having the urge to binge or to purge. Not dieting means that I now enjoy a basically normal and healthy relationship to food, a belief that food is no big deal. Most importantly, not dieting means that I have never, of my own choosing and with my own hand, applied the hatred of fat to my own body using the ritual of a diet. Although I've had to fight for happiness as a fat person, I've had a much easier time of it than my friends, whose repeated dieting embedded the self-hatred under layers of shame. (Self-inflicted wounds are often the hardest to renounce and forgive.)

If dieting is largely hereditary, then perhaps parents can help change that inheritance. One of my mother's favorite quotes comes from the musical *South Pacific*. It goes, "They have to be carefully taught." The quote is about racism and how people learn it as children. It is an optimistic quote that assumes we are born without hatred, just like we are born without credit card debt. Then parents say the most commonplace things: "Don't eat that cookie, you'll get fat" or "Don't tell the lady she's fat; that's not a nice thing to say" or "Tell me, does this dress make me look fat?" Our children are carefully taught.

Percentage of dieters who
REGAIN THE WEIGHT WITHIN THREE YEARS: 90
Percentage of Americans who believe in miracles: 70

Fat children get extra lessons when their parents—with the best of intentions—put them on diets. The parents don't want their children to be teased. They don't want their children to have health problems. The child doesn't see a diet that way. All the fat child knows is that she gets teased at school for being fat, and instead of her parents protecting her from that trauma, they basically agree with her bullies and take away her food. Now the child is unhappy *and* hungry. The message children get from such parental intervention is this: "If you're fat,

there's something wrong with you. We'd love you more if you were thinner." Frankly, after talking to dozens of fat adults who were forced onto diets in their early years, I think the child's got it right.

Parents may need to do a bit of rebelling of their own to protect their kids from fat hatred. My dear friend Haley Hertz was labelled as fat *in utero* by doctors who put her pregnant mother on diets. Despite this, Haley weighed a healthy six pounds six ounces at birth. The doctors decided to put her on diet infant formula, though, because they decided she had too big an appetite. ("Gee, maybe I was hungry because I was starved in the womb," Haley says.) According to UCSF endocrinologist Dianne Budd, M.D., parents who deprive children calorically during the first year of life risk permanently affecting the child's ability to sense when she is full. Children are born with the ability to know when they are hungry and when they are full. These cues are the basis of the body's weight-regulating mechanism. Kids who diet mess up that mechanism.

Sure enough, my friend graduated from infant formula to an endless string of weight-loss attempts: Weight Watchers, behavior modification, predigested liquid protein fasts,

PRINT SOME FAT-POSITIVE SLOGANS ON MAILING LABELS AND STICK THEM TO DIET PRODUCTS AT THE GROCERY STORE.

OptiFast, an OptiFast look-alike called Complement, Nutri-System, the UCLA teen diet program, Overeaters Anonymous, diet pills, diet shakes, diet candies, diet puddings, diet teas, the gastric bubble (which Haley said came along just in time to save her from an even worse fate: stomach stapling), a smorgasbord of low-calorie diets, high-fiber diets, low-fat diets, high-carbohydrate diets, pure protein diets, fruit-only diets, boiled egg diets, cabbage soup diets, bananas-and-skim-milk diets, and every other fad diet that came along.

Despite her mother's efforts to make her lose weight, or perhaps because of them, Haley is still fat. Here's what she has to say about growing up like that:

All of my life, I felt that there was something inherently wrong with me. I wasn't allowed to eat the same things that my sisters got. They got substantial food, and I got raw vegetables and skim milk. I was never allowed to eat bread. I used to say that even prisoners got bread and water. My parents never said that I was beautiful. They said that I could be beautiful. They never said that I was perfect. They never said that I was good. I never felt like I would ever be good enough. Everything in life that I ever wanted was withheld until I was

thin. When I lose weight, I can have some pretty clothes. When I lose weight, I can take dance lessons. When I lose weight, I can be human. The message was clear. Being fat made me inherently bad, ugly, and unlovable. The funniest part of all is that back then, I wasn't really fat. I just believed that I was.

If you're a parent of a fat child and you don't want your child to be teased, then do something to put an end to the teasing. Your child probably isn't the only one suffering. If you want your child to be healthy, don't obsess about food. The best advice from the experts is that parents should provide good, nutritious food. Then let the child decide how much to eat. That's right, let the child decide. When parents restrict food

Do the double chin! It's double the fun!

115

or push food, kids just learn to ignore their own feelings of hunger or fullness, yet these feelings of hunger and fullness are exactly what allows the body to maintain its healthy, natural weight. In other words, it's counterproductive to try to control what a child weighs.

Here's how exercise physiologist Glenn Gaesser, Ph.D., puts it: "The chances of a fat kid getting slim are about the same as the chances that if a kid eats like Kareem Abdul Jabbar, he'll grow up to be seven feet tall and play in the NBA."

On the issue of exercise, the experts do say that parents should encourage children to do physical activities they enjoy: dancing, riding bikes, playing a sport, etc., but they warn that forcing children to exercise will just make it into a punishment the children will want to avoid.

If your parents taught you that it's bad to be fat, you can reject that lesson in your own life. And you don't have to pass self-hatred down to your children. Unhappiness doesn't have to be hereditary.

DESERTS

by Kristine Durden

My sister's talking hesitantly
as we drive that familiar highway
through the colorless valley
She pauses, embarrassed, irritated
You don't act like you're fat, she says
You act like it doesn't matter

I laugh, shocked
My sister, the beauty queen
thin like a ruler
pale blue in her love
wants me to bemoan my bigness
thinks it will be better to be depressed

The large beige hills pass by us
A mass of land, rounded mountains
made useless by drought
And how should I act? I ask her
waiting to see what she'll say
wondering if she'll yell out
Stop being happy
having sex, enjoying food
living your life as if fat
doesn't matter

CHILDREN CAN BE SO CRUEL

EVERY ONCE IN A WHILE, I GO BACK TO school. I go back to college, high school, sometimes even junior high. I only go back for an hour, actually just fifty minutes, but while I'm there, I tell students stuff they've probably never heard before, stuff that I certainly never heard during the seventeen-odd years that I spent in classrooms.

When I go back to school, I tell young people to use the F-word. I get us all to say it out loud together: fat. Then I explain who I am and why I'm a fat rights activist. I tell them that it really is okay to be fat, that you can be happy and healthy at any size, that you don't have to lose weight to get a life. I say that, since people naturally come in all sizes, it's not okay to be mean to those of us who happen to be fat. Most importantly, I talk about what it feels like to be comfortable in your skin, to like who you are and how you look. At first, they look at me like I'm crazy, but they also hang on every word. Their worries start to come out. They want to talk about Barbie dolls and eating disorders and *Seventeen* magazine. They ask me tough questions like these:

* Were you ever so unhappy about your weight that you wanted to kill yourself?
* My mom is always dieting and it drives me nuts. What should I say to her?
* I don't like my body the way you like yours. What am I supposed I do?

I give the best answers that I can. Slowly, they all start to realize that if I can stand up for fat people, then they can stand up for themselves —that none of us has to feel bad. I leave school so excited—because I know how much it would have changed my life if *any*one had spent even five minutes saying this kind of stuff to me when I was young.

Here's what some high school students had to say about me and my message, after I talked with them:

* I learned that nobody has the "wrong" body size. I think this information is controversial and correct.
* I think she is right, but it is hard to let go of beauty standards taught since birth.
* I felt she was 100 percent correct, but I still couldn't shake away the feeling that I do not want to be fat.

WHENEVER YOU SEE ADS FOR DIET PRODUCTS POSTED ON TELEPHONE POLES AND WALLS AROUND TOWN, RIP THEM DOWN.

* I've never been overweight, but I do get pressure (from my mom) to keep slim or else!
* I learned that no matter what your body size is, if you're okay with who you are and if you lead a healthy lifestyle, there's *nothing wrong with you.*
* The statistics about diets and discrimination were unreal.
* You don't have to change who you are to fit a

mates started teasing him about his weight. The teacher was on hall duty, just outside the classroom. Brian said, "I'm tired of it!" He pulled out a gun and shot himself in the head. He was sixteen years old. Friends later said that Brian had been teased since he was in junior high.

Tragically, Brian's case is not the only one.

In 1996, twelve-year-old Samuel Graham hung himself from the tree in the backyard of his

CHILDREN who had leukemia SAID THE WORST PART
wasn't the pain, or the chemo, or the possibility of dying—it
WAS BEING TEASED BY OTHER CHILDREN
for not having hair.

Spice Girl mold. I can't tell you how thrilled I am to hear of this.
* I'm a thin guy, but now I feel reassured about my weight, and I hope our talk can improve my insecurities.
* I hope you are able to speak to many more groups about this issue.

I started giving these talks when I first heard about a fat teen who committed suicide. It happened in 1994. Brian Head was a high school sophomore in Georgia. One day, he was waiting for his econ class to begin, when some class-

family's Florida home. He was supposed to start middle school the next day, but he couldn't face the prospect of being teased as the fat kid. Samuel's two younger brothers were the first to notice the body. His father refused help from emergency personnel, retrieving his son's lifeless body himself.

In 1997, an English girl named Kelly Yeomans took a fatal overdose of painkillers. She was thirteen years old. For three years, she had suffered taunts about her weight from a group of teenage boys. During the week before her suicide, the bullies gathered every evening to throw butter and eggs at her family's house and shout about "smelly" Kelly. Kelly told her parents, "It's nothing to do with you, but I can't stand it. I'm going to take an overdose." Her parents thought she was depressed, but never dreamed she'd go through with the threat. The next morning, she was dead.

These are just the cases we know about. There's no telling how many more fat kids out there are feeling just as desperate. What I do know is that no fat child makes it to age eighteen unscathed by teasing.

I can recall every single time that I was teased for being fat. It probably happened to me less than a dozen times, but it had a lasting effect on my self-esteem. For a long time, the taunts I received colored my hopes for the future. I don't want that to happen to any more fat children. I simply don't want any more fat children to die.

We cannot expect individual fat kids to rise up courageously and silence their tormentors any more than we expect children of color to defend against racist comments all by themselves. Our opposition to fat hatred should be just as vehement, just as immediate, and just as certain as our opposition to racism. I know it

may seem scary to speak up. If it scares us, think how fat children must feel.

If you want to do something to protect fat children, if you want to do something to help children of all sizes feel better about themselves, contact the Kids Project at the National Association to Advance Fat Acceptance: (800) 442-1213. The Kids Project educates teachers about fat prejudice and trains volunteers to give talks in schools. I believe so strongly in the need for this program that I'm donating half my proceeds from this book to help support it. The Kids Project needs your help, too—your support, your participation, and your ideas. I hope you'll join me in making the world a safer, happier place for fat kids.

O IS FOR OKAY

"I don't think I'm any less appealing or sexy or funny because of my weight. I see these shows on anorexia, and women look in the mirror and think they're fat. I am kind of fat, and I look in the mirror and I don't think I'm as fat as I am. But I don't have self-loathing because of it."
—Rosie O'Donnell

A NORMAL CHILDHOOD

by Tracy Pekar-Rogers

T SEEMS TO ME LIKE MY CHILDHOOD WAS THE exception to the norm. I was a fat kid, and a working-class one at that. So not only did I have the fat issue to deal with, I also could not afford the designer blue jeans and name-brand shoes that were so important.

I am adopted, and both my adoptive parents are very thin. But weight just wasn't an issue for me. I was fed healthy, balanced meals, and junk food was not readily available in my household, but it wasn't banned, either. The general consensus was, as long as I was healthy, I was okay.

I don't remember having much crap to contend with in elementary school. Sure, there were kids that picked on me, but there were precious few who never got picked on at all. I was able to realize that they might pick on me 'cause I was fat, but they picked on Mike 'cause he had braces, and Mary 'cause she was not allowed to wear sneakers, and Shaun 'cause his mom gave him a green apple every day in his lunch.

In junior high and high school, I never had much trouble at all. I was one of the biggest girls in school, but it was just never an issue. Maybe one or two kids called me size-related names. But I always came right back at them with something against them. (I was not an easy target and was generally left alone.)

Why was it that way for me? I am not sure. But I think it had a lot to do with the attitude I was raised with. I was constantly told that I was important, and there was nothing I couldn't do, and to hell with those who didn't agree. I guess a healthy disrespect for authority contributed to it. Some would label me "cocky," some "rude." But, by God, I had my own opinion, and to me it was the only one that mattered. (Notice I say "mattered" not "right.")

My husband is a fat person, nowhere near as large as myself, but "overweight" nonetheless. Will I have kids? Hopefully. Will they be fat? Probably. Is this a moral dilemma for me? Not particularly. To me, the importance of raising a child outweighs any anxiety over mistreatment that child might receive if that child is fat.

P IS FOR PERFECT

"Food has replaced sex as a source of guilt."
—*Psychology Today*

"What some call health, if purchased by perpetual anxiety about diet, isn't much better than tedious disease."
—George Dennison Prentice

"A fat woman is a quilt for the winter."
—Punjabi proverb

Beauty is in the eye of the beholder, and it may be necessary from time to time to give a stupid or misinformed beholder a black eye!"
—Miss Piggy

THE WEIGHT QUESTION

I F THERE WERE A FAT HOMELAND SOMEWHERE on the world map, we might not have this problem. If there really *had* been a golden fat era, when fat was worshipped, we wouldn't be in this bind. (I'm sorry, but a couple European painters and one prehistoric statuette don't constitute a golden era.) If fat children were only born to fat parents, and thin people only came from thin families, then our glorious fat heritage, passed down through the generations, might save us from this situation. As it is, there is no official language of fat pride. There are no fat slang words, no fat neighborhoods, no fat holidays, no traditional music of the fat people. There is no comforting and familiar fat cuisine, no special dance that fat people dance when we are happy or sad, no fat hairstyle, no rite of passage for fat children to undergo (other than the teasing). There is, in short, no fat culture.

Now, black culture and queer culture and Jewish culture and deaf culture, to name a few, are sources of support and identity and pride for the people who belong to them, and these groups speak a common language. Meanwhile, individual fat people rarely even have the words to refuse our oppression, much less a language with which to express and celebrate our own experience. Instead, when we want to talk about our condition, we end up parroting the very words that the mainstream culture uses to keep us down. We say, "I need to do something about my weight problem," when what we really mean is, "I want this discrimination and mistreatment to end."

Although there is not yet a fat culture, we do have a fat community: fat organizations and newsletters, books and magazines, conventions and parties, clothing stores and dating services, and thousands of people who either create these resources or use them. Given that the mania for thin only really flourished in the last 100 years, and given that fat people only started to resist that mania in an organized way about twenty-five years ago, we have accomplished a lot. Still, fewer than one tenth of one percent of America's ninety-seven million fat people are out of the closet and actively enjoying fat community. Yet the closet is no safer or happier a place for fat people than it was for gays and lesbians. The fat closet, like any closet, holds the dangers of unlived life, self-hatred, teen suicide, and brutalizing, futile "cures." Despite these very real dangers, fat people are staying in the closet because they cling to the false hope of one day passing for thin and because there is not yet a fat culture to welcome them home, to welcome us home.

Don't worry. It's coming. If just 1 percent of fat Americans came out of that closet, we could start to make the mainstream nervous. If a mere 5 percent of fat Americans used the F-word with pride, we would begin to generate a culture of our own. If one tenth of fat Americans came out—nearly ten million strong—we could put a serious dent in the diet industry's ability to profit from our oppression. If one fourth of fat Americans (about twenty-four million of us)

rejected the shame and the self-hatred, we could successfully lobby for laws to protect us against weight-related discrimination on the job. If one third of fat Americans came out, we could start our own chain of fat-positive fitness centers nationwide, or found our own fat-friendly HMO. (With thirty-two million members, it'd easily be quadruple the size of Kaiser Permanente. Ha! How's that for *fat* health?) If half of all fat Americans took a stand against prejudice, we could colonize the state of California as the new fat homeland. If three quarters of fat Americans were out of the closet, there would be TV sitcoms with all fat actors, comfortable chairs in every public location (including airplanes), and Oprah would hire a cook and a trainer to help her regain the weight. If all ninety-seven million fat Americans celebrated their luscious selves with pride, the statement "Fat Is Beautiful" would be self-evident. Children would have to ask their parents what *dieting* means and would look at them in horror when they heard the explanation. Modeling agencies would hire on thousands of beautiful young women and men of all sizes to satisfy the public's new, inclusive aesthetic. Doctors would discover that body fat protects against many diseases, but is otherwise harmless. Women, both fat and thin, would

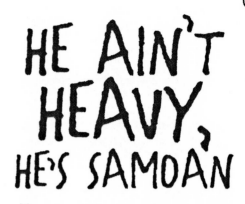

start making huge advances in business, politics, science, and the arts, using all the energy and ambition they previously devoted to worrying about their weight. People would refuse to say "overweight," referring to it instead—in hushed, apologetic tones—as the O-word. Fat people would lead normal, happy lives, full of the usual mix of love, work, family, friends, and car payments. And on National Fat Day, everyone, fat and thin, would slick their hair back, don the traditional orange-and-hot-pink kilts, and take to the streets in the fat parts of town to dance the belly bossa nova until dawn. Fat culture, here we come.

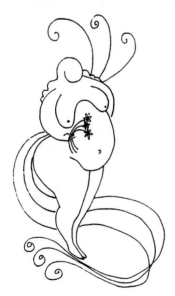

HE AIN'T HEAVY, HE'S SAMOAN

A T ONE POINT IN THE MOVIE *PULP FICTION*, the characters played by Samuel Jackson and John Travolta are trying to recall some guy they both know who is half black and half Samoan. One says, "Oh yeah. Fat, right?" The other says, "I wouldn't go so far as to call the brother fat. What's a *n*—— gonna do? He's Samoan." Then the conversation drifts off somewhere else, in its arty, *Pulp Fiction* way.

This scene sticks with me, however, because I think a lot of fat people would like to be Samoan. We don't really mind being fat, and we don't want to be thin. We're just tired of the whole question. We would rather be Samoan. Now, Samoa is a small cluster of islands. I doubt that it can support the reverse diaspora of ninety-seven million fat Americans. But we can all be Samoan in our minds. To that end, I've written the following, third-grade-style report

123

about Western Samoa. My information comes from the brilliant Margaret Mackenzie, Ph.D., associate professor at the California College of Arts and Crafts, an anthropologist whose life

to keep the wind out. People eat taro root and coconut, fish, a kind of spinach, and sometimes canned corned beef from New Zealand. Fruits and flowers grow everywhere—frangipani and

Fat people are regularly excluded from testing to be bone marrow donors.

THERE IS NOTHING WRONG WITH A FAT PERSON'S BONE MARROW. The standard device used to extract bone marrow is simply too short to work on fat people.

work concerns the meaning of body size. Professor Mackenzie did field work on nutrition, body size, and aging, in a small village in Western Samoa in the 1970s, and it is to that village that I propose we travel in our fantasies.

MY REPORT ON SAMOA

Geography: Samoa is divided in two parts, American Samoa and Western Samoa. My report is about a remote village, in Western Samoa, called Lalomalava. Lalomalava is located on the shore by a lagoon.

Culture and customs: In the village of Lalomalava, the men and women all wear sarongs and thong sandals. They live in houses on raised platforms with thatched roofs and no walls. In bad weather, people use woven mats

orchids and hibiscus. The flowers are used for greeting and for saying farewell. Different flowers mean different things, depending on their colors and how rare they are.

Government: People in Lalomalava spend their days cultivating their fields, fishing, getting water, making tapa cloth, and engaging in village politics. Both women and men can be chiefs, but everyone gets involved in making decisions. People in Lalomalava think that Americans don't know very much about politics, because we don't have very good ways of settling disagreements. They're also not very interested in the United States, because they believe their culture is superior to ours.

Health: Six hundred people live in Lalomalava. They are Samoans. Many Samoans are fat.

124

The average woman in Lalomalava is five-feet four-inches tall and weighs 200 pounds. In Lalomalava, it is not good or bad to be fat; it just is. The men in Lalomalava think the women look good the way they are. No one in Lalomalava has high blood pressure, and fewer than 1 percent of the people get diabetes. Compared to the women in Lalomalava, women their size in the United States have much higher blood pressure and get diabetes much more often. Samoans who live in Hawaii or on the mainland are not as healthy as Samoans in Lalomalava, either.

Exercise: Everyone in Lalomalava sits on the ground, not in chairs. Because of this, the people have no trouble trimming their toenails. In fact, the Lalomalavans are some of the most flexible people in the world. Lalomalavans don't do aerobics, but everyone walks every day, and people in the village love to dance a slow, rhythmic dance. If you are fat there, that's no reason not to dance.

What Lalomalavans say to researchers who study weight and health:

* "Our country has some serious problems, and here you are studying body size. Why don't you study something important?"
* "Now look, this stuff about body size. . . . If you don't want to get fat, don't get married.

Everyone knows that every time you get pregnant you won't lose the weight. By the time you have seven or eight children, you'll be fat. That's the beginning and the end of it."

And that is my report on Lalomalava. I think it sounds very nice to be a Samoan.

Q IS FOR QUEEN-SIZE

"Fat—bottom girls you make the rockin' world go 'round!"
—Queen, a rock band

BMI: BOLD & MEANINGFUL INFOR- MATION ABOUT FAT

by Sondra Solovay

* Number of weight control services in the Oakland, California, Yellow Pages: 55
* Number of battered women's shelters in Oakland, California, Yellow Pages: 1
* Cost of getting liposuction on just one area of the body: $2,000 to $4,000
* Hourly income for performing digestive organ reconfiguration (a weight-loss surgery): $4,687.50

125

* Yearly spending per student in Utah public schools: $2,967
* Percentage of U.S. high school students who drop out each year: 27
* Percentage of Americans who call education one of the most important problems facing the country: 3
* Percentage of Americans who are "very concerned" about saturated fat: 61
* Circulation of *The New York Times*: 1,145,890
* Circulation of *Weight Watchers* magazine: 1,006,397
* Percentage of American women who avoid wearing a bathing suit: 88
* Percentage of people who are satisfied with their health: 88
* In the average population, number of people per million who have primary pulmonary hypertension, a frequently fatal disease: 1 to 2
* Number of people per million who took Fen/Phen for more than three months who have PPH: 46
* Number of vitamins whose absorption is prevented by Olestra: 4
* Percentage increase in risk of hip fracture for a 150-pound woman who loses fifteen pounds: 280
* Percentage of people who fully recover from hip fractures: less than 50
* Percentage of women who say they diet for their health: 21
* Earnings for commercial weight-loss programs in 1991: $2 billion
* Percentage of enrollees in those programs who were women: 95
* Average difference betweeen a fat woman's annual household income and that of a thin woman: –$6,710
* Percentage increase in likelihood that a woman will live in poverty if she is fat: 10
* Percentage of the 3.8 million people with incomes over $75,000 who are men: 87
* Number of dollars American businessmen sacrifice in salary for every pound they are "overweight": $1,000
* Twenty-year-old Kate Moss's earnings from runway work alone in one year: $2,000,000
* Average annual salary for a sixteen-to-twenty-four-year-old woman who works full time: $13,350
* Spending on ab machines in 1996: $400,000,000
* On any given day, number of American women on diets: 30,000,000
* On any given day, number of Americans who are hungry: 30,000,000

THEY CALLED ME HANK

OUR CULTURE IS SO WEIGHT-OBSESSED that even babies aren't exempt. Go to any Hallmark shop and try to find a birth announcement that *doesn't* have a place to fill in the newborn's weight. I dare you.

Even at that tender age, weight means something. Underweight babies are cause for worry. Average-size babies fall into a narrow range, from six to eight pounds, labeled "normal-healthy." Then, above eight pounds, folks start to whistle or groan or cluck when they say, "Now, that's a big baby."

When I was born, I weighed nine pounds and seven ounces. I was healthy. I was big. People clucked. My birth weight even inspired my first and most enduring nickname. The story of how I got this nickname is one that my parents have told for as long as I can remember. On my mother's side of the family, there's a traditional name, Henry. When I was born, my father thought I should have the middle name Henrietta, to continue that tradition in my generation. Mom thought that was a great idea. My parents called the North Carolina relatives, including Uncle H. M. (the *H* stands for Henry). When my dear Uncle H. M. got the exciting news of my birth, he said, in that loving-joking Southern way, "At nine pounds seven ounces, that's no Henrietta. That's a Hank!"

From the time I was three or four years old, I knew I was fat. I don't know how I knew. Perhaps I'd heard the story of my nickname. Perhaps I'd noticed that when adults lifted me they said I was heavy. Perhaps I simply soaked up the knowledge that something made me different and that difference had to do with size. I wonder when other little children realize they are black, or disabled, or different in other ways. I imagine that knowledge comes to us early on. What kind of survival skill is it, that little toddler brains learn the ambient prejudices, even as the toddlers are forming their first words?

Thanks to my rather unfeminine nickname, I've always known that, even though I was different and would simply never be one of the thin, popular, lace-ruffle-ankle-sock kindergarten girls, I had something else: the swashbuckling, rebellious persona of a Hank. I haven't always worn that nickname publicly, but it always comes out at times in my life when I've been at my most adventurous or genuine: when

HECK, POSE FOR SOME NUDE PHOTOS. IT'S INCREDIBLY EDUCATIONAL.

I'm with family, when I entered college, when I started *FAT!SO?*. It makes me happy, proud even, when someone calls me Hank.

Here's a suggestion for Hallmark. Instead of having a line for weight on birth announcements, offer a space to fill in the infant's nickname instead. It's much more useful information.

GENERATION XXX

EVER SINCE WOMEN WORE BLOOMERS, hippies wore tie-dye, and drag queens wore evening gowns, clothing has been political, even revolutionary. This is just as true, perhaps especially true, for fat people.

For too long, we have have allowed the number on a tag to define our lives. How do you first know that you've crossed a line and become a fat person, anyway? You don't fit in the thin sizes or in the thin department or in the thin stores. It's like a big "Thin Only" sign marks certain territory off-limits.

What you wear says something about who you are, and what you *get* to wear determines, in many ways, who you get to be.

Well, fat people are no longer trapped in the polyester double-knit prison that suffocated us for so long, thanks to an incredible boom in the market for fat fashion. The large-size clothing market for women has grown from $2 billion in the eighties to more than $10 billion in the nineties. Back in 1978, there were just 100 makers of clothes for fat women. Now, there are more than 1,200 companies that cater to us. Forty percent of American women wear a size 14 or larger. All of this means that fashion designers are looking at fat women with new respect—for our money, and, increasingly, for our beauty.

I say it's time to claim all those Xs. They're the mark of a radical, revolutionary, outsider chic. We're at the start of Generation XXX, and we can claim the power of clothing and use it to encourage flabulousness for our fat sisters and brothers.

The next step is to develop our own flabulous style. We can take the funky clothes that are available now in our sizes and make them our own. Take the blue vinyl car coats, the faux furs, the silk suits, the gowns that are revealing rather than concealing, the fantasy lingerie, the little skirts. Take all of it. We can grow into that flabulousness by wearing the clothes, even if we don't feel flabulous at first. We'll make it our

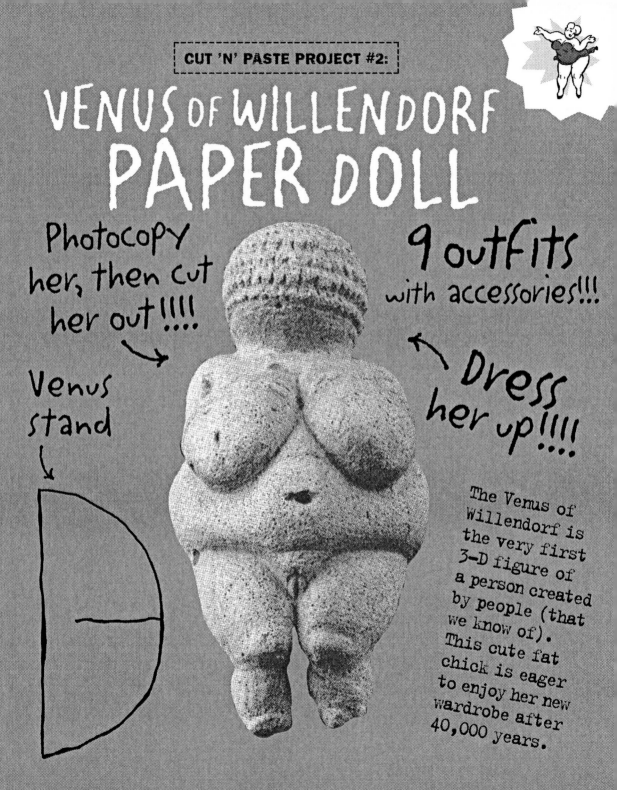

CUT 'N' PASTE PROJECT #2:

VENUS OF WILLENDORF
PAPER DOLL

Photocopy her, then cut her out!!!!

9 outfits with accessories!!!

Venus stand

Dress her up!!!!

The Venus of Willendorf is the very first 3-D figure of a person created by people (that we know of). This cute fat chick is eager to enjoy her new wardrobe after 40,000 years.

Black
leather
jacket—
it's so
groovy!

HITTIN' THE HIGHWAY!

Bikini power!

AT THE BEACH

Every
Venus
needs
lingerie
and a
feather
boa.

IN THE BOUDOIR

Do the Dashiki.

AT THE PROTEST RALLY

Love those Docs

BOY

AT THE BOOKSTORE

Ms. Goddess

You can put sequins on her evening gown!

AT THE PAGEANT

AT THE LUAU

What color is your bandana?

BREAKIN' BRONCOS

own. Then we'll be ready to demand even cooler clothes from those same designers next season.

Some new size labels would help mightily in this process. It's a shame that so many women (and men) start feeling bad about themselves when they start wearing the fat sizes, especially since that line keeps moving. Is it a size 16? A size 14? A size 12? If you live in LA, fat is a size 8! Yet the average American woman is five-feet four-inches tall, weighs 144 pounds, and wears a size 12 or 14.

back corner of the uppermost floor to find our area, which is bizarrely called the Women's Department. (What? A size 8 isn't a woman? Isn't that kind of insulting all around, for thin and fat women alike? Kinda damned if you are, damned if you aren't?)

Why not insist on sizing terms that reflect the actual measurements of the person they're intended to fit? This system works wonderfully for men and allows them to walk into stores, locate a shirt or a pair of trousers by number,

---

The corset of a **FASHIONABLE WOMAN** in the mid-1800s exerted up to eighty-eight pounds of pressure. Her wintertime clothing weighed thirty-seven pounds, with **NINETEEN POUNDS OF CLOTHING** suspended from her waist alone.

How would we feel about ourselves if, instead of numbers like 12 or 14, those labels simply read, "Average"? Then, larger sizes would be "Above Average." I'd hate to call my thinner sisters "Below Average," so I'm sure we could come up with some sort of euphemism: "Pre-Average," "Averagettes," "Girls"? No, that doesn't seem fair. Even though, for years, flabulous fat women have had to ride up and up the department store elevators and trek to the far

and buy it without all the calisthenics of a session in the fitting room. But I'm not sure women are ready to claim their true measurements. Until that honest day, flabulous fashion-heads can do something even better. Forget all the numbers. Ignore them. They no longer apply to you. Why should you accept the label of a system that puts you down? Become, instead, a member of Generation XXX! (Add as many Xs as you fancy.) And may all your fashions be XXX-cellent.

REFUSE TO APOLOGIZE FOR YOUR SIZE.

MY SIZE

by Debora Iyall

Newspaper ink on my fingers
Morning milky taste in my mouth
From wet sidewalk to
Hot department store

Up the escalator I pass
Beds that aren't beds
The lingerie department has gone
    white wicker,
Unmentionable garden

I search for my usual rack

A sales lady ignores me, wraps
Lacy purchases,
Crisply pulls carbons from a
Credit card receipt

She says
"We don't carry your size."
So I said
My size does not need to be carried.
My size danced all night then
Swam in the Gulf
All morning

I'm like you, lady,
From marrow to eyelash, but more so
And I don't apologize
For my size

CLOTHING THAT CHANGED MY LIFE —OR— CELEBRATING YOUR INNER BIKINI

WHEN I WAS IN THE SIXTH GRADE, I WORE a size 14/16. I don't think my mom was ready for her daughter to start wearing women's sizes. What to do? At about that time, my mother read some helpful-homemaker article in a women's magazine about a way to make caftans out of sheets. You just cut the sheet in half, made a neckhole, and sewed it up the sides. Remember the rainbow sheets? The Vera sheets with the lime green fern fronds? The Star Wars commemorative sheets? I wore them all. Please understand, my mother was not being intentionally cruel. She wore these caftans herself. It was the seventies. I'm sure stranger things were happening than moth-

150

er/daughter bed linens as outerwear. It may have been self-defense, but I don't think I realized just how strange these caftans were at the time. It's a wonder that I had any friends at all, billowing as I did. But I did have friends, good ones. Those caftans marked the first time that clothing would change my life. I learned that I could overcome anything, that my personality really is more important than my looks, and that conformity is the easy way (but definitely not the best way) out.

The next piece of clothing that changed my life was a black suede vest. Until this vest, I had always refused to go sleeveless, no matter how hot the weather. Like so many people my size, I believed that my upper arms were too fat for public viewing. Then one night, not long after I bought this vest, an acquaintance invited me to a concert, a band called Einstürzende Neubauten. It's a German group that uses power tools and metal the way some bands use guitar and drums. This acquaintance warned me that, because of the molten lead, it might get hot during the show. So I decided to wear the vest, buttoned, with no shirt underneath. This meant baring my arms, but I thought, "Hey, people at an Einstürzende Neubauten show can hardly complain." As it turned out, we had to

wait outside the club for an hour, while the musicians did an exacting sound check on their rivet guns. While we stood in the warm summer night, I asked my acquaintance whether my arms looked too awful, whether I shouldn't have covered them up. She was simply surprised at my question, and said, "No, of course not. They're lovely and round." That was all it took—a flat statement from a disinterested party. It was all I needed to reclaim a body part that I'd been hiding in shame for decades. And you know what? My arms *are* lovely and round. In fact, all of me is. What's more, it feels good to wear sleeveless things and feel the air on your skin. Not long after that, I reclaimed my knees, too. I started delighting in miniskirts and little short flirty dresses, bike shorts, and all sorts of fashions above the knee—more to the point, above *my* knee, my cute little dimply round knees that don't deserve to be hidden away from the world, my knees that never did anything to harm anyone.

In recent years, so many clothes have helped me feel flabulous: the zebra-stripe Lycra bodysuit with orange feather boa and orange platform shoes, the pink ruffle-butt bloomers worn over leggings and under a big sweatshirt, the Italian suit coat in rich chocolate brown with

SOAK NAKED IN A HOT TUB WITH A BUNCH OF FRIENDS.

the perfect leopard-spot scarf, the little black dress in the sproingy fabric.

The most life-changing and political garment of all is a swimsuit that I commissioned from a fat seamstress friend. The event that inspired it was the annual gathering of the fat people (a convention sponsored by NAAFA) and, specifically, the gala pool party that takes place on the first night of this weeklong event. I decided this pool party would be the perfect place to demonstrate, as much as possible, my refusal to be ashamed of any of the lovely round parts of my body. Inspired by the popularity of *Baywatch* and the fad at the time for wetsuits, I asked the lovely April Miller to design a bikini for me. It's black, a zip-front crop top with a mandarin collar, cap sleeves, and hot pink piping, and it has a thong bottom. I wear this suit with the distinct variety of pride that one can only experience whilst wearing a thong bikini during the pool party at a convention of fat people. And like the pool party itself, my thong suits have become an annual tradition, much-anticipated in some circles. I can't imagine now why I stopped wearing two-piece suits after age seven, or how I did without them for so long. I've read that nearly 90 percent of American women avoid wearing any kind of bathing suit, much less a two piece.

I can only say to those women, "Jump in, the water's fine." Clothing isn't just for looks anymore. Bikinis *are* political. Your wardrobe can indeed change your life.

SHOPPING WITH MOM

by Johanne Blank

POPPED INTO THE LOCAL TJ MAXX THE OTHER day, to browse the shoes and the plus-size racks, just on the off chance that there would be something there that called out my name. A very thin, expensive-looking mom was in there with her probably thirteen- or fourteen-year-old daughter who was fat. Mom was looking revolted, daughter was looking perfectly miserable, and I overheard mom saying to daughter, "You see what will happen to you if you don't go on a diet like the doctor told you? You'll end up looking like *that*."

I (dressed in a rather smashing straight black skirt and black silk tunic, a big gorgeous russet-and-gold Indian scarf, and my most decadent hat) turned to Mom and said, "Pardon me,

TRY A WATER AEROBICS CLASS. IT'S A GREAT TYPE OF EXERCISE FOR FAT PEOPLE.

but just what is wrong with the way I look? Do I have lipstick on my teeth?" Mom stammered.

"Or," I ventured, "were you making a remark about my weight?" Mom didn't say anything.

I turned to the daughter and said, "Look, don't let your mother tell you that being fat is going to ruin your life. It isn't. I know better. Being fat is just one of the things that people are, like being Jewish or being black or being gay or being bald. Don't listen to your mother when she tries to make you feel bad about yourself, okay?"

Mom grabs her daughter by the arm and announces that they're leaving.

I said, "Excuse me, ma'am, did I offend you by talking to your daughter?" Mom is red-faced and clearly furious.

"I'm sorry if I undermined your attempt to shame your daughter in public, ma'am," I said, doing my best Eddie Haskell impersonation.

I walked away, and then turned around to see the daughter still looking at me. I flashed her a thumbs-up sign and blew her a kiss and walked out of the store, shaking and furious but feeling like I did the right thing.

It's the first time I've ever confronted someone in public like that (at least someone *else's* mother). I always wished someone would've stopped and said something to me when I was that thirteen-year-old kid being embarrassed in public by her mother, so I just kinda let fly. I rather doubt I would've been quite so vocal had it not been for being exposed to all the wonderfulness *chez* Hank. We've shared too many stories of too many childhoods stained by parents being bigoted and abusive for me to feel like not saying anything would be a good thing, y'know?

I really do hope that what I said makes a dent for the kid. I remember with vivid ghastliness the shopping voyages with my mom as a child—and I remember the marvelous sense of freedom when I was about fourteen and I managed to save up enough money from baby-sitting and odd jobs to go into the upscale women's sizes shop (though I was all of a size 18 at the time) and buy myself a sweater and a pair of pants that I actually liked, with no parental interference, no one giving me *tsuris* about my size. I haven't gone clothes shopping with my mother in a *long* time. Life's better this way.

DON'T BE AFRAID TO BE SEEN IN A SWIMSUIT.

GAB CAFÉ
SUCCESS STORY #3:
THE ENTREPRENEUR

CATHY MILLER WASN'T PLANNING TO QUIT HER job and start her own business when she first visited Hank's Gab Café on the *FAT!SO?* Web site (www.fatso.com). But she did have an idea.

She stopped by the clothing topic in Hank's Gab Café to try her concept out on the Gabsters:

I make flowing tops and jackets out of washable rayon Indonesian batiks that I pick up at Southern California swap meets. So far, *order. I might be nuts, but there are so few really reasonable, really knockout clothes out there for us. I want to share the wealth!*

The response was overwhelming. So many Gabsters wanted her sarong-wear that Cathy decided to start a business. She called it Big On Batik. In her first nine months, Cathy made and sold 300 batik pieces to women of all sizes.

One Gabster's husband (a professional photographer) loved his wife's new batik outfit so much he took photos of her wearing it and gave them to Cathy to use in her first brochure. Cathy's daughter also contributed some beautiful drawings. Now, Big On Batik has customers all over the world.

For some customers, Cathy's batiks make a huge difference in how they see themselves:

In a 1977 study, half of the LANDLORDS REFUSED TO RENT AN APARTMENT TO A FAT APPLICANT. All of the landlords were willing to rent the same apartment to a thin applicant.

I've only made them for myself and a few close friends. Our big bodies make a beautiful canvas on which to drape these exotic artworks. I'd love to sell these garments by mail- *I got a note from one woman who hadn't been out of her house in quite a while. She was embarrassed about her size. But she bought a batik from me and wore it on her*

first trip outside. Thanks to that, she decided
she was going to buy some more nice clothes
so she could leave her house and feel good
about herself. When I read that, I just sat
down and cried.

Cathy now sells her wonderful sarong-wear
at gatherings of fat people around the country.
She shows women how these brightly colored
clothes not only celebrate fat pride but also
keep up with our busy lives. "I tell people that a
batik jacket over black pants and a simple shell
is career wear. Over a bathing suit, it makes a
great beach cover-up. And worn over nothing at
all, it's sure-fire sex!"

THANK YOU, BARBIE!

HAD A BIG PILE OF BARBIES WHEN I WAS
young. People worry about the example this
doll sets for girls. But sometimes, as in my case,
Barbie was a much-needed antidote. You see, I
never once thought that I could be Barbie. Ever.
We just didn't have enough in common, looks-
wise. Yet Barbie was my idea of what it meant to

Chances that a woman has
THE "IDEAL" BODY: 1 IN 40,000

be a grown woman (despite the evidence of all
the grown women around me—my mom, teachers, family friends, women in the grocery
store—none of whom looked like Barbie any
more than I did). Since my chubby self could
never resemble Barbie, I never imagined myself
as a grown woman. I never planned on having
the kind of life I imagined a Barbie-style grown
woman would have: marriage (to some guy
who's a bit stiff but who looks good in a suit),
kids, a career in the helping professions, a town-
house, a battery-operated dune buggy, self-
inflating swimming pool, cone-shaped artificial
breasts, a special carrying case to hold all my
clothes, and lots of high-heeled plastic shoes.

Instead of those things, I explored the real
world, met all kinds of odd people, and developed my own quirky sense of style and
lifestyle—and I have Barbie to thank for it. She
saved me from a life of conformity and bland-
ness. Whew! Thank you, from the bottom of my
heart, Barbie.

USE YOUR BUOYANT FAT TO FLOAT BLISSFULLY IN A POOL ON A SUNNY DAY.

WHY YOU SHOULD DYE YOUR HAIR HOT PINK

* Because hot pink is the new fashion neutral.

* Because it's nothing to be afraid of; it's just a little box of hair color.

* Because being fat sets you apart from the crowd. But being fat *and* having hot-pink hair makes you flabulous.

* Because Dennis Rodman isn't the only cool rebel on the planet.

* Because little kids will love you for it. They'll say, "Mommy, look at the lady with pink hair!" instead of, "Mommy, that lady is fat." Better still, they'll believe you when you tell them that being fat is cool.

* Because it's several thousand times cheaper than weight-loss surgery, and it'll make you feel several thousand times better about yourself—without leaving a nasty scar (or causing permanent damage to your internal organs).

* Because you'll attract butterflies and hummingbirds and other cool rebels like yourself.

* Because it matches your eyes.

* Because whenever someone looks at you funny, you won't have to wonder why.

* Because when someone asks you how your hair got pink, you can look them in the eye and say, "It's natural."

* Because you can't be fired for having hot-pink hair if you say it's part of your religion.

* Because it really *is* part of your religion.

* Because you want to start the fat revolution.

* Because hot pink matches your personality.

* Because you only live once, and bungee jumping just isn't your style.

* Because waking up in the morning, looking in the mirror, and seeing yourself with hot-pink hair will wake you up faster than a shot of espresso. And it'll do more for your self-esteem than a year of therapy.

* Because then your hair will match your lingerie and your socks.

* Because just think of all the people who will smile when they see you.

* Because bringing so much joy gives you tons of good karma.

* Because I got a fortune cookie once that said:

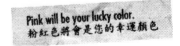

Pink will be your lucky color.
粉紅色將會是您的幸運顏色

WHEN YOU MEET UP WITH A FAT FRIEND, TRY BUMPING BELLIES INSTEAD OF HUGGING HELLO.

R IS FOR RIGHT SIZE

"Genetic inheritance is much more important than people currently think. We have never found any twins in which one was extremely lean and one was extremely obese (sic). It simply doesn't happen. No matter what they ate as children."
—Dr. Susan Roberts, a researcher at Tufts University's Jean Mayer USDA Human Nutrition Research Center on Aging

"There are 3 billion women who don't look like supermodels, and only 8 who do."
—Ruby, a beautiful, fat, nine-inch fashion doll depicted on a promotional poster from the Body Shop

TRY BUMPING BELLIES IN PARTING, AS WELL. IT'S A FUN WAY TO ENJOY YOUR LUSCIOUS BODY.

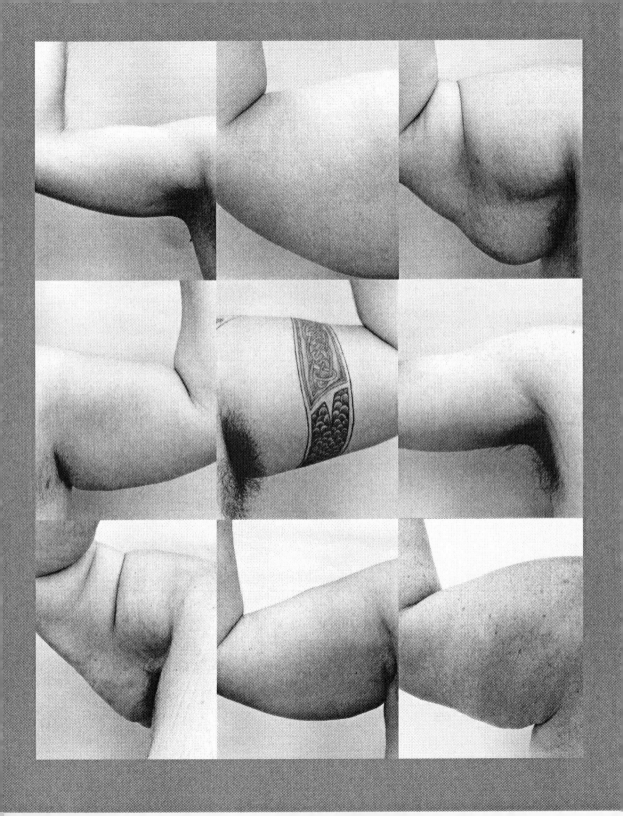

ANATOMY LESSON #4

THE UPPER ARM

MUUMUU-
OF-THE-MONTH
CLUB
(A FATLIN MINT EXCLUSIVE)

RELIVE THE NOSTALGIA OF YOUR DAYS AS AN oppressed fatso. Harken back to the years of double-knit peasant blouses and vertical stripes. Celebrate the ultimate symbol of fat fashion with this Limited Edition of Twelve Heirloom-Quality Collector's Muumuus.

Muumuus celebrate the special beauty of fat people everywhere. Descended from a classic lineage that includes the Roman toga and the stately kimono, the modern muumuu offers a look that goes from the bedroom to the board-room to evening wear. Don't hesitate to invest in this wearable art that's practical, too. Unisex styling makes muumuus a wardrobe basic for the whole family.

The talented artisans at Fatlin Mint have expertly stitched the distinctive seasonal themes for these glorious caftans. As a proud member of the Muumuu-of-the-Month Club, each month you will receive a muumuu adorned with intricate, individually handcrafted details, from the flashing lights of our Christmas muumuu to the Scratch 'n' Sniff pumpkin-scent panels cleverly concealed in our October muumuu.

160

Created by acclaimed muumuu artist Phoebe Billow exclusively for Fatlin Mint, these garments meet our exacting standards. Phoebe controls every stage of the sewing, and each muumuu bears the artist's signature under the left armpit. This Fatlin Mint limited edition will be closed forever after just seventeen sewing days.

Your elegant muumuus of 100 percent polyester sateen are completely washable. They are as lovely to wear as they are to display proudly in your home. As part of your club membership, you will also receive a wall-mounted display unit in either genuine brass-esque finish or authentic wood-look.

Keep the enchantment of the seasons close to your person forever with an heirloom muumuu. Available exclusively by reservation from The Fatlin Mint for just $49.95 a month. (If you don't absolutely love these muumuus, simply burn them on a pyre in your backyard. Or hand them down to a chubby niece or nephew. We sure as heck don't want them back.)

S IS FOR SATISFACTION

"Do you know the two things I like about Richard Simmons? His face."
—Tom Snyder, on his show, "The Late Late Show with Tom Snyder."

"Everybody hates to hear how hard it is to be beautiful, but I can tell you that because of the way I look, I know people are watching my lips move and aren't hearing what I'm saying. It makes you understand prejudice."
—Cybill Shepherd, actress

"I find a lot of people like chubby 67-year-old girls."
—Beverly Sills, opera star

WHEN IN RUSSIA...

BACK IN 1991, I WENT TO RUSSIA FOR A month. I got there just after the tanks left Moscow, when Boris Yeltsin took over the government. It wasn't an easy place to be, but for some reason I felt incredibly confident and happy there. I saw some amazing things and made some good friends in Eastern Europe, but this good feeling went deeper than that. When I landed at Heathrow Airport on the way home, I realized why.

In Russia, I saw no advertising, window displays, fashion magazines, movies, or TV shows. Aside from a quick visit to the McDonald's on Pushkin Square, I wasn't exposed to marketing of any kind for four whole weeks. I didn't see a photo of Cindy Crawford or an ad for Weight Watchers or a billboard for diet Coke. When I went to the *banya* and beat myself with birch leaves, the other women in the steam room looked more or less like me. In Russia, the only reminder of my appearance was the bathroom mirror.

At Heathrow, I faced rows of gleaming duty-free shops. After my time in Russia, the choices were daunting and, in subtle ways, damaging. I browsed among souvenir T-shirts that didn't come in my size, perfumes advertised by thin models, magazines that touted the seven secrets to a flatter tummy. Everything reminded me of what I wasn't; my mood drooped. In the spartan Moscow Airport, just a few hours earlier, I had been a satisfied traveler, mulling over my recent adventures. In Heathrow, I was a dissatisfied consumer, prey to dubious luxuries.

I hope it's not necessary to sacrifice self-esteem for selection, but what about the choice of simply being comfortable in one's own skin?

I learned a lot about American culture in Russia. I learned that, in America, the pressure to conform is so pervasive we hardly notice it's there, constantly wearing us down. I recommend taking the occasional vacation from this pressure. Once you escape its pull, conformist culture can never grip you quite as firmly. If you don't feel like going all the way to Russia, then please accept a souvenir from me: It's a small, imaginary lacquer box with a painting of a beautiful fat woman on the top. Inside it is the knowledge that you are fine, just as you are.

T IS FOR PRESIDENT WILLIAM HOWARD TAFT

"Just as a man and a real honest-to-God fellow, Mr. Taft will to his grave with more real downright affection and less enemies of any of our presidents . . . He was our great human fellow because there was more of him to be human. We are parting with 300 pounds of solid charity to everybody, and love and affection for all his fellow men."
—Pundit Will Rogers' obituary for 27th U.S. President William Howard Taft

"Thou art the cosmic bulge,
   the overspill;
Thou art America,
   Brobdingnagian Bill."
—*Punch*

A GOOD FAT RANT

by Joanna Iovino

AM FAT. I WEIGH OVER 350 POUNDS, SO I HAVE experienced firsthand the effects of fat discrimination in our society. Fat people are seen as lazy. Fat people are considered stupid. People think that all we do all day is sit around eating bonbons and watching Ricki Lake.

I have to assume that people also think fat people have no emotions, because I don't think they would say the things they do if they saw us as human beings with feelings and thoughts similar to their own. I have had people yell out their car windows at me. It is as if they feel it is their duty to inform me how fat and ugly I am. Uh, excuse me, I have a mirror at home, I am quite aware of my size.

But those aren't the worst people. The ones that I hate even more are the people who just stare as I walk past them, and who whisper words of pity to their friends. I don't need pity. I am a fully functioning human being who just happens to be in a larger package than most.

And then of course, there's the, "Oh you have such a pretty face, if only ..." club. That gets on my nerves! As if I could be broken down and defined by my individual features, rather than as a full person!

And employers: I don't even want to discuss the trouble I have finding a job. People are not willing to hire large women. Large men are often seen as powerful, large women as lazy and stupid. When the ad says, "Must have professional appearance," I don't bother to apply. By "professional appearance," they mean "thin, pretty, and fashionably dressed." Although I don't see how being thin would enhance my job performance!

Oh, and one more thing. For some reason, men seem to think that fat women are desperate sluts willing to sleep with anyone just to get some. Uh, no I don't think so. We are looking for the same qualities in a man that any other woman wants. Just because we are fat does not mean that we will accept any old unemployed, cheating bum. Believe me, there are plenty of quality men out there who appreciate a large woman.

Before you go off and make comments about fat people, remember, we are fat *people*. That means we are human and have the same feelings and emotions as anyone else. Please respect that.

163

FAT PHRASEBOOK

I F YOU'RE PLANNING TO TRAVEL FOR ANY extended period of time in that exciting psychological realm called fat pride, you'll want to brush up on some of the common words and phrases used by the people in that state. It's amazing how learning to speak just a little bit of the language can help you have the time of your life. A word of caution: Don't worry if these phrases are a bit hard to pronounce at first, or if the accent sounds odd to your ears. You'll get the hang of it.

ON A DATE/WITH A ROMANTIC PARTNER

* Have you ever dated a fat person before? I just want to find out whether you know how much fun you're in for.
* If you're not comfortable being seen with a fat person, then I can assure you, you won't be!
* Of *course* I know the belly bossa nova!
* No, I don't want to share a dessert. I want one of my own. But I'll happily trade bites with you.
* That's okay. I'd rather leave the lights on.

WHEN SOMEONE IS RUDE

* Oh dear, what ever gave you the idea that your opinion matters?
* (and tall) I'm not overweight, any more than you're overheight.
* (looking directly in their eyes) What did you say? (Hold their gaze. Make them be the first to look away.)

ON A JOB INTERVIEW

* You may have noticed that I am fat. I realize that when some employers interview fat applicants, they have concerns about physical ability, sick days, and corporate image. I can assure you that I would not have tendered my resume if I were not certain that I can perform this job in a superlative manner.
* One of the reasons I would like to work at Amalgamated Widgets International is the company's reputation for valuing diversity in its workforce. Such a forward-thinking organization benefits not only from employing people of different colors, ages, genders, and religious backgrounds but also from employing people of all sizes. This is especially true given that fat Americans represent one half of the population and are therefore also one half of Amalgamated's pool of potential

MAKE SURE YOUR PTA, YOUR N.O.W. CHAPTER, YOUR HEALTH CLUB, YOUR UNION, YOUR POLITICAL PARTY, AND YOUR PLACE OF WORSHIP ARE ALL SAFE PLACES FOR FAT PEOPLE.

employees and one half of its customer base. Such inclusive practices can only inspire my loyalty toward this company.

IN THE DOCTOR'S OFFICE

* The chairs in your waiting room are inaccessible to fat people. Please provide a chair without arms, so I will be able to sit down when I arrive for my appointment.
* No, thank you. I'm not willing to be weighed.
* You will need to use a larger blood pressure cuff to get an accurate reading.
* Could I have a larger gown? This one looks like a paper napkin on me. (What? You don't have any large-size gowns? Please order them from NAAFA at 1-800-442-1214.)
* Doctor, I came to you with a health complaint. Your suggestion that I lose weight is not a satisfactory response. If you saw a thin patient with the same complaint that I have, what treatment would you recommend?
* You want me to diet, doctor? Why would you recommend a treatment that has a 90 percent failure rate?

These are just some beginning phrases. Don't hesitate to make up your own.

U IS FOR UMOJA

"To reaffirm faith in fundamental rights, in the dignity and worth of the human person, in the equal rights of men and women and of nations <u>large</u> <u>and</u> <u>small</u>." (Emphasis added.)
—charter of the United Nations

V IS FOR VALEDICTION

"You are not as fat as you imagine. ... Enjoy your body. Use it every way you can. Don't be afraid of it or of what other people think of it. It's the greatest instrument you'll ever own. ... Dance, even if you have nowhere to do it but your living room. ... Do not read beauty magazines. They will only make you feel ugly."
—A widespread e-mail rumor attributed these immortal words of advice to a 1997 MIT graduation speech given by Kurt Vonnegut. The speech never happened; Mary Schmich wrote this in a *Chicago Tribune* column.

GO TO YOUR LOCAL DEPARTMENT STORES AND LOCATE THE LARGE-SIZED CLOTHING SECTION.

ROSEANNE SIGHTING

THE WAITING: IT'S 9:30 A.M. ON A SATURDAY, and I'm standing in line behind about thirty people on the concrete shopping cart ramp outside Costco waiting to see Roseanne, who is signing her new book, *My Lives,* at noon. I am behind Howard and Fidel, gay flatmates who watch a double header of Roseanne reruns every weeknight. Howie just took the bar exam, so he's a bit keyed up. He spends the entire two-and-a-half-hour wait thinking up obnoxious things to say to Roseanne and asking us how he should have her sign his book. By noon, the line does several laps across the roof of the parking garage. The crowd is young trendies, middle-aged suburbanites, gays, groups of lesbians in their best T-shirts, people of all colors, the occasional fatso like me, families, and a lot more men than you'd expect.

The meeting: I'm nervous, but Howie is channeling all the hyperactivity in the place, so I look calm. It's my turn. I hand Roseanne a hot-pink *FAT!SO?* flier along with the book she's going to sign. She starts reading the flier. She reads the part where I ask folks to send me stories about their own Roseanne sightings, and I say, "Yeah, if you know anyone who's seen you in a Burger King, give them my number." She laughs. Score! She seems a bit shy of the crowd scene, but she totally gives off the reflected power of all these cool people who came to see her today because she's a nexus for something they all want—the ability to set aside pretense and say what's what. Roseane shakes my hand, but I'm so disoriented I can't even make eye contact. I forget to ask her what her favorite fat joke is. At the checkout line, I'm behind Fidel and Howie again and we're all grinning. Howie says, "I didn't say anything to her! I just told her how much I love her."

The moral: When I get home, I want to call everyone I know, but I just sit by the window instead, feeling this jolt. What is it? Roseanne puts regular people into her show, people who go to work and get cranky and get by, who might be fat or gay or black or poor or whatever. It's acceptance, and it's powerful. People need it so much. We are so beautiful when we get it and so grateful to anyone who really offers it. I hope Roseanne feels that acceptance herself. She deserves it. Next time I see her, I'll try to calm down a little and look her in the eye, because that's all it takes.

IF THE LARGE SIZES ARE HIDDEN IN A BACK CORNER ON THE TOP FLOOR BEHIND HOUSEWARES, ASK THE STORE MANAGER WHY THEY DISCOURAGE FAT CUSTOMERS.

W IS FOR WONDERFUL WOMEN

"A diet counselor once told me that all overweight people are angry with their mothers and channel their frustrations into overeating. So I guess that means all thin people are happy, calm, and have resolved their Oedipal entanglements."
—Wendy Wasserstein, Pulitzer Prize-winning playwright

"A woman has all too much substance in a man's eyes at the best of times. That is why men like women to be slim. Her lack of flesh negates her. The less of her there is, the less notice he need take of her. The more like a male she appears to be, the safer he feels."
—Fay Weldon, author

"Too much of a good thing is wonderful."
—Mae West, actress

"I feel my responsibility as a successful English actress is to say to all those young women who are out there in turmoil about their weight—'Life is short, and it's here to be lived.'"
—Kate Winslet, actress

"Dieting is the most potent political sedative in women's history; a quietly mad population is a tractable one."
—Naomi Wolf, *The Beauty Myth*

"One cannot think well, love well, sleep well, if one has not dined well."
—Virginia Woolf, *A Room of One's Own*

CALLING ALL FAT MEN

WHEN I TALK ABOUT THE THINGS THAT concern fat people, I'm not just thinking of fat women but also of fat men. Certainly, fat men are not exempt from our culture's craziness about body size. It's no easier to be fat on Mars than it is to be fat on Venus. It's just different. Fat boys have the fun of playground fights, of "Husky" jeans, and of being assigned by some sadistic PE coach to play on the "skins" team in basketball. Fat men get to multitask their body anxieties: hair loss, penis size, and hey, while you're at it, look at that belly.

That's why it makes me sad to see so few fat

men at the fat-positive events that I attend. It's not only because I think y'all are incredibly good-looking and handsome and all that. (I just

your fat sisters, do it for your own selfish reasons, too! For all the reasons that are unique and important to fat men.

In a study of 10,000 people in their early twenties, researchers found that

FAT MEN WERE 11 PERCENT LESS LIKELY TO BE MARRIED, and fat women

were 20 percent less likely to be married than their thin counterparts.

---

consider that a bonus.) I'm guessing that fat men might really like to hang out with other fat men, trading war stories, ranting against the ills in our society, and strategizing the fat revolution. It might be reassuring, a bit of a relief, a source of brotherhood. (Now, fat gay guys already have a wonderful and extensive network. And these lads are definitely freedom fighters, in the sense that living well is the best revenge.) I still miss my fat brothers, because I don't think fat liberation will happen without you. It's an unfortunate, sexist phenomenon, but as long as people think of fat as a women's issue and a question of vanity, they will continue to disregard the seriousness of antifat prejudice. As it is, fat women have been fighting that prejudice for a long time. We could sure use some help. But don't just join the fight to help

If you're a fat man, and you want to enlist in the fight for fat freedom, just call me up at (800) OH-FATSO and leave your number on my machine. (Heh heh heh.) I'll get in touch and let you know how to get started. (Wink, wink, nudge, nudge!)

BY ANY MEANS NECESSARY

NOT LONG AGO, THE NATIONAL ASSOCIATION to Advance Fat Acceptance received the following inspirational letter, which is reprinted here with the kind permission of its author. While the fat liberation movement has yet to develop a military wing, when and if it does, fat brothers like John Latham will be ready.

Greetings from Louisiana!

I am not a member of your organization, but I think you will be happy that I have taught people to accept my fatness. Every day that goes by, someone new learns to accept the fact that I am fat.

I weigh 529 pounds. I am twenty-four years old. I have been fat since I was in junior high school. For years people have called me names like Big Butt, Big Fat John, and Fat Head, just to name a few.

Within the last year, I have learned an effective way to get people to accept me as a fat person. Now when someone calls me a name, I beat them up. I beat them up real bad. I have been arrested three times because of it, but that is okay because I sent those people to the hospital.

I can hit skinny people real hard. I can punch a hole through a wall. I'm real tough and mean. Now when someone looks at me wrong, I beat them up. I beat people up everywhere. I've beaten people up at malls, grocery stores, and high school football games. Now people are afraid of me. They're afraid of me because I'm tough and mean, and I can beat them up real bad.

Please tell all your association members about my new method of getting respect for us chosen fat people. People that call us names need to be beaten up. If you would like, I can come to you and teach you some fighting moves to beat people up in the same manner that I do.

Thank you for reading my letter, and I trust you will get back to me very soon.

Thanks again. Sincerely,

John Latham

LEARN HOW TO KICK-BOX.

X IS FOR EXECRABLE

"We pass through this world but once. Few tragedies can be more extensive than the stunting of life, few injustices deeper than the denial of an opportunity to strive or even to hope, by a limit imposed from without, but falsely identified as lying within."

—Stephen Jay Gould, *The Mismeasure of Man*

JOIN THE AIR FORCE, SEE THE SCALES

by Porter Bennefield

AM A FORTY-NINE-YEAR-OLD MAN. I HAVE always been on the edge of what was deemed by others to be overweight. I graduated from high school in 1967 and enlisted in the air force. I ended up making the air force a career and retired from active duty in 1987. My retirement ended twenty years of frequent weigh-ins. At 183 pounds, I was within 10 percent of the Air Force's maximum weight limit. I was required to weigh in twice a year, instead of just once a year. I was also called in to be weighed by every inspection team that came to the base where I was stationed. And I was subject to no-notice weigh-ins, as well. I remember living in fear of these weigh-ins. I remember not eating or drinking at all on days when I knew that I would have to weigh in. I remember taking diuretic pills for a week or more in order to meet the limit. I had to weigh in if I wanted a base transfer. If I weighed too much, I couldn't get the transfer. What I weighed occupied my thinking on an almost daily basis.

Everyone had theories on how to reduce weight quickly. One captain's theory involved raising the body's temperature to increase water loss. I remember sitting in saunas to sweat off enough water to get safely below the weight limit. (And by safely, I mean safely below the limit, not safely losing the weight.) To make matters worse, there was always a slight difference between the scale in the gym and the scale used for weigh-ins. In order to sweat off enough water to ensure I was below the weight limit on both scales, I had to ignore the time limits posted outside the sauna. I always felt light-headed and dizzy after a weigh-in.

One time, I realized that the ruler used to measure our official height was inaccurate. I

LEARN HOW TO FLY AN AIRPLANE.

challenged it, and they had to admit that I was taller than they had said I was.

I'm amazed that after almost ten years of retirement, I am only now learning how much the fear of being over the weight limit dominated my life and the emotional and physical toll it took on me. Over the years, I developed negative feelings about my body. I still have these feelings, although I feel better about it now that I've found fat-positive groups and individuals. The feeling I get from the fat community is such a relief that it's hard to describe. I feel joy at finding there are so many other people who have had this experience, that I'm not the only person who's felt this way. Now I feel like I'm part of a larger family that I didn't know existed.

TALES OF A FAT LAD

by Charles Van Dyke

ALWAYS GOT BEAT UP AS A CHILD. THERE WERE two teenagers who loved to use me as a punching bag. Once when I was about ten, one of them started hitting me. A group of adults gathered around us and cheered him on. I fought back as best I could, but at ten, I did not have the strength of a seventeen-year-old. He hurt me and I started crying. That is when an adult stepped in and broke it up. This so-called adult told me, "You were doing fine until you started crying." Such compassion!

In grade school, I also had three classmates who liked to gang up on me. I learned how to vary my route home, which garages were open, or where there were places to hide. Once these classmates and the teenagers caught me on the way to school. They started throwing rocks and bricks. I will say that I did get a few tosses back at them, but there were too many of them. They hit me several times, once on the head. I was lucky that someone came out of a house and chased them off. I finished walking to school, not knowing that blood was pouring from a cut to my head. The teacher/nurse who patched me up asked me what I had done to make them so upset.

I learned to catch my classmates at school, where I could grab one of them at a time and use my size to an advantage. The problem was that the first time I did this, the rage and hate I felt was so strong that I wanted to kill the boy. It took two adult teachers to pull me off him. The principal gave me a long lecture on how I almost killed this boy and if I did not control my temper I would kill someone. This did have an effect on me, as I never wanted to kill anyone. From then on, I never fought unless I knew that there was someone who could stop the fight before I really hurt anyone. Of course, this was usually at school, but it did have the effect of stopping the beatings outside of school. They knew I would pick them off one by one, when I had the advantage.

I even played basketball in the fifth and sixth grades. I had to put up with the locker-room abuse, which the coach thought might motivate me to "lose some of that lard." This sent a message to my teammates that I was fair game for any kind of fat joke. I had some strengths at basketball. I was a lot faster than they expected a fat kid to be. I played forward and led my team in the number of stolen balls and jump balls.

In high school I was labeled a troublemaker. It was okay to pick on the fat kid by putting gum on the chair. It was okay to ruin one of his two pairs of pants, to hit the fat kid and run, or just make fun of the few clothes his parents could afford to buy. I gave them an answer that they did not expect. I am not proud, now, that I chose to attack them physically. At that time, it was the only solution that seemed to work. The school counselors would just say it was my fault and tell me to go on a diet. There was no support from adults. I had to take things into my own hands.

It is worse for fat children today. We have to stop this misguided obsession to make everyone look the same. People will vary in size, weight, color, etc. A lack of tolerance, for any of those differences, shames all of us. We need to teach children to take pride in the gifts and talents they are given and let them become all that they can. I hope that, soon, no more children will be driven to suicide because of fat hatred. I want them to have a better childhood than I did.

Tony with spare tires

DIAL-A-CLUE

If you enjoy watching *Wheel of Fortune*, reading your horoscope, jiggling a Magic Eight Ball, or throwing the *I Ching*, you'll love Dial-A-Clue. The little spinning arrow of fate isn't just for meal choices any more. It's for attitude, too! In fact, there's no need to feel bad about your weight, when thrice-daily use of Dial-A-Clue is sure to keep you on the fat-friendly path. It's easier than ever. Now you can make your very own Dial-A-Clue. Just copy this portentous pinwheel onto heavy paper at your friendly neighborhood copy store, assemble it, and clue yourself in.

INSTRUCTIONS: Cut a small hole at the dot in both the arm and the
wheel. Attach the arm to the center of the wheel using a brad.
(I love that word!) Spin the arm to Dial-A-Clue.

FLIRTING 101

"**A**RE YOU A FLIRT?" MOST PEOPLE ANSWER no. (Watch out for the ones who answer, "Oh no, not me. I'd *never* flirt." They're doing it already.) Fat people, especially, will protest, saying, "I can't flirt at all. I'm really bad at it." (What's *that* about?)

How to explain, then, the fact that there's a whole bunch of flirting going on? *Someone* must be doing it. It can't possibly be just a few, very busy, very flirtatious people out there having all the fun.

In fact, I think I can pinpoint the unaccounted-for flirting activity. It's coming from fat people. We flirt all the time, without realizing it. We flirt for survival. We flirt because, otherwise, people might not even notice we're here. We're extra friendly, so people will like us. We turn on that jolly, charming, ingratiating attitude just to make sure that folks recognize we are human beings and treat us accordingly. This flirting requires great subtlety, because narrowminded individuals are prone to being spooked by the thought that

a fat person is flirting with them. Sadly, because we flirt all the time, we don't notice the effort it takes and often fail to realize our own incredible skill. What's worse, fat people all too often discount our own flirtworthiness. This is a bad habit we pick up from a fat-hating world and the bizarre propaganda that seeks to deny how attractive, sexy, and desirable fat people are. Luckily, you can easily shake off such an unhealthy attitude simply by flirting more and flirting like you mean it!

Since you are most likely already a flirt, this instructional segment will simply offer a limbering-up exercise and a few pointers designed to help you stay aware of the flirting you're already doing.

First of all, flirting is like any other martial art. The first thing you must practice is how to take a fall. In judo, the instructor accomplishes this lesson by flinging students down onto padded mats. With flirting, taking a fall means looking foolish. If you're not afraid to take a fall—i.e., look stupid—that's half the battle. So, to begin, we will practice the traditional warm-up exercise in looking foolish. We will sing

---

PUT ON A FASHION SHOW WITH YOUR LOCAL LARGE-SIZE CLOTHING STORES.

the Junior Birdman song—with witnesses. I use this exercise when I lead flirting workshops, and it never fails to prepare people to do their best flirting ever. If you're trying this at home, just find an audience of at least one person (the more the better) and sing the following words to them while performing the gestures diagrammed below. (If you don't know the melody, just make one up—the sillier the better.)

THE JUNIOR BIRDMAN SONG

Up in the air Junior Birdman
Up in the air upside down
Up in the air Junior Birdman
And keep your tail feathers off the ground!

Now that you have limbered up by making yourself look as foolish as possible (without using any unusual props), you are ready to take on any flirting situation. Just remember. Flirting is its own reward. Should you meet someone who doesn't flirt back, assume they have a toothache (poor them), and move on. Finally, some pointers to keep in mind.

TOP TEN REASONS TO FLIRT

1. To get discounts and freebies
2. To obtain secret spy information
3. To avoid boredom, or to pass the time
4. To receive untold riches
5. To make the world a better place
6. To avoid standing next to the bean dip all night looking foolish
7. To have fun
8. To reassure yourself that people are basically nice
9. To feel flabulous
10. To meet people (and, if you insist, to get dates)

TOP TEN REASONS FLIRTING FAILS

1. You're not really interested in flirting; you just want to get laid.
2. You flirt as if you were walking a tightrope, and you keep forgetting not to look down.
3. You're afraid the other person won't take you up on it.
4. You're afraid the other person *will* take you up on it.
5. You're not that funny after all.
6. Your left eye is twitching from the strain of acting casual.
7. You pick the wrong time to flirt: when the cop pulls you over, on a sinking boat, at a funeral.

176

8. You flirt in monologue, not dialogue.
9. You let the other person do all the talking—about mutual funds.
10. You don't speak French.

CLASSIC FLIRTATIOUS OPENERS (OR AT LEAST, ONES THAT WORK FOR ME ...)

1. Hello! (The best line of all time.)
2. Isn't this a lovely tomato?
3. Oops! (People invariably look, some may even offer help.)
4. Is it hot in here?
5. Young man, you make my mouth water.
6. Would you like to help me feed the ducks? (Requires a park with a lake, some ducks, and some bread slices, as props.)
7. Is this seat taken?
8. Are you a friend of the bride or the groom?
9. Would you hold my spot in line?

And the all-time classic . . .

10. Do I have lipstick on my teeth?

THE JOYS OF FAT SEX

IF YOU'RE AT ALL LIKE ME, YOU TURNED TO THIS section first. That's cool. This is as excellent a chapter to start with as any. Besides, one of the first and most inaccurate assumptions people make about fat folk is the one about us being unsexy. Nothing could be further from the truth! So I'm glad we're getting that misunderstanding cleared up right away. And just because you're reading the sex chapter first, that doesn't mean I'm feeling any twinges of performance anxiety. Oh no! (Well, not all *that* much, anyway.)

First, let me just say that I don't have the secret. If there really is some secret to sex, then I kinda doubt it's going to be revealed to the world on page 177 of a book for fat people. But then, you never know. Maybe the secret you're looking for is here. (And hey, if you already know the secret, go write your *own* book!)

Instead of a typical sex secret, I'd like to give you some reassurances. I think you'll actually like them better. With a secret, there's always the danger that your legs won't bend in that direction. With reassurances, you actually get to feel better about your sex life, rather than worse—plus, you're not likely to pull anything. (Well, not anything you don't want pulled.) Okay, enough foreplay, I'm eager to get into the joys of fat sex, of which there are just so very, very many. The following reassurances (and joys) are culled from discussions with dozens of

mean fat people can't get some, too. You don't need to attract everyone at the party, just the one good one. Confidence makes you sexy, not control-top pantyhose. Fat women are actually more orgasmic than thin women (according to a study by *Weight Watchers* magazine, of all places). When someone says you look good, they probably mean it; don't protest, smile, and say thanks. "More to love," is not just empty propaganda; a fat person can touch you, cuddle you,

PERCENTAGE OF AMERICAN WOMEN WHO SAY THAT FEELING FAT HAS MADE THEM AVOID SEX: 25

lovely, friendly, sexually active fat people. Admittedly, this list is not complete. I encourage you to go out and find more items to add to it! Until then, enjoy . . .

Sex is more about skin than it is about muscle tone. If one position doesn't work, there are at least twenty more that do—and they're probably more interesting. Fat people do not suffocate, crush, deflate, squash, or break their partners. It just doesn't happen. You can *so* get on top. Everyone jiggles, that just means you're doing it right. There is no sex shortage. Just because thin people are getting some, doesn't

embrace you, in ways no thin person ever could. Sometimes an armful is more fun than a handful. One of the ways fat people overcompensate is by developing what the pros call technique. It ain't what you've got; it's how you use it. Hard bodies are nice, but soft bodies are nicer. If you hate your thighs, you make it tough for anyone to love them. If you love your thighs, you make it tough for anyone to hate them. The same goes for your butt and your belly, too. The sex is better when you use all your parts. You *are* sexy, damn it! Stop having sex with people who don't believe that. They don't need your charity. In nature, whales and cows and elephants and pigs and hippos all enjoy thriving sex lives—what great role models! Thin people have dry spells, too. Fat people make great float toys—think about it. Speaking of toys, get one. They're guaranteed to come in your size; heck, get several, so you can share when your friend(s) come over to play. Big bellies make really good canvases for body painting—or for spelling out naughty suggestions in Gummi alphabet. Just because there's never been a great fat sex scene in a movie doesn't mean you can't star in your own. Your largest sex organ is your brain, and it's about 10 percent fat. (Hey, they say we only *use* 10 percent of our brains at any one time.)

(Many thanks to all the fat folk who contributed ideas for this chapter. You know who you are.)

A NEW POSITION ON FAT JOKES

by Cynthia Meier

T IS LATE NIGHT, AND WE ARE WATCHING DAVID Letterman. Tired and tense after a long day, I think that maybe some zombie time will relax me. I know better; TV is too easy. I know it's bet-ter to take a long bath by candlelight, better to read or write, or even dream about our next vacation. I know better.

But the button on the remote control touches so easily, and I can justify that David Letterman is a social gauge of our world—an improvisa-tional artist worthy of my time. I can justify almost anything.

We tune in in time for Letterman's Top Ten List. Tonight, he is talking about Roseanne. A rumor was circulating that Roseanne and then-husband Tom were marrying a third person, and this caught Letterman's attention. I have since for-gotten everything on the list—a barrage of fat jokes. I forgot all of them except one. One of Letterman's Top Ten Reasons to Marry Roseanne and Tom was so they would have someone to operate the winch on their honeymoon.

My face stung with indignation and embar-rassment as I saw the words scroll across the screen. I felt the world's eyes turning to my bed-room. I clutched my lover's hand as we watched, and I felt my face harden. We went to bed with this embarrassment between us.

Several days later, on a Sunday morning, my lover and I are dawdling in bed, making love. As we switch from one position to another, my leg gets caught under me. We laugh and struggle a

ENCOURAGE YOUR FRIENDS AND LOVED ONES TO STOP DIETING.

bit to maintain our balance. As we negotiate our position, I suddenly realize that what we need is a winch—and somebody to operate it. I say this, and we both start to laugh. We remember the embarrassment and outrage of the other night, and we laugh some more. We feel our laughter lighten us and move us closer. It also helps us find the right, new position.

I still reflect on this. David Letterman's joke was not well-intended or even good-natured. I still believe it was cheap and cruel. But I'm also aware of a transformation in me, a change that allows me to accept a joke made at my expense and transform it. Instead of guarding so carefully, I'm aware of embracing and accepting a little more. Maybe this is what fat power is all about: transforming the enemy's weapons and even realizing that there is no enemy. Perhaps Letterman was speaking from personal experience! I don't know what all the implications are for accepting fat jokes, but I do know that rigidity is not the right position for me. I can laugh at myself and maybe the world, and find a place of expansiveness in both.

IN PRAISE OF APPETITES

NOT TOO LONG AGO, WE HAD JUST AS MANY taboos about sex as we now have for food. Sex was sinful, more often than not. Excessive interest in sex was a serious no-no. Having sex for pleasure and not just for procreation was deemed immoral and self-indulgent. Nowadays, food is the sin. Eating more than you "should" is a big no-no. Using food for pleasure, not sustenance, is considered just as self-indulgent—even immoral—as a libertine's lifestyle once was.

A hundred years ago, health experts urged the public to restrain sexual appetites in such classics as J. H. Kellogg's pamphlet *Chastity and Health* (1895), the premarital primer *The Moral Elevation of Girls* (1885), or the article entitled, "Some Thoughts on Personal Hygiene and the Waste of Life's Forces Through the Emotional Nature" (1896). We look back and titter at such Victorian sex literature now, just as people will certainly look back, 100 years from now, at the diet books of the late twentieth century, and laugh at our effort to deny another appetite: the natural, human appetite for food.

STAND TALL AND PROUD. THROW THOSE SHOULDERS BACK. DON'T SLOUCH OR HANG YOUR HEAD.

To prove my point, I've taken some quotes from current diet books, but replaced all the food and weight-loss words with equivalent, sex-related terms. If these passages seem ridiculously antisex, perhaps that just reveals how ridiculously antifood the originals are.

* "Conquer your cravings for sex once and for all! . . . The doctor tells you exactly how much sex to have and when to have it, a simple plan that will regulate your hormones and keep you in control of your urges."
  (*The Five-Day Miracle Diet*, by Adele Puhn, M.S., C.N.S.)

* "Finally, celibacy without deprivation!"
  (Rave review for *The Carbohydrate Addict's Diet*, by Rachael and Richard Heller)

* "I hadn't always suffered from a lust problem. During my childhood and early twenties, I considered sex a necessary function—not the focal point of my life. . . . In college I was always on the go with very little time to have sex at all. . . . As far as I was concerned, having sex was a nuisance I could do without. I would never have imagined that I could gain so much libido and lose control of my sex habits, but that is precisely what happened. Years later, I found myself at the opposite end of the spectrum, compulsively stuffing my body with sex, look-

ing forward to every encounter, and craving all types of sexual pleasure."
(*Free of Dieting Forever*, by Janet Mills)

* "I have learned that lust is a chronic medical condition that needs regular treatment and management for life . . . The desire to lose that extra lust remains part of the American psyche, with half of the population—and as much as 70 percent of American women—currently restricting their sexual intake in an effort to become more chaste."
  (*Thinner At Last*, by Steven Lamm, M.D.)

* "Never feel horny again! . . . You can never eliminate sex completely. But how much is too much?"
  (*The McDougall Program for a Healthy Heart*, by John McDougall, M.D.)

* "Sex may be the most powerful drug you will ever come in contact with. But you can learn how to control your desire for it!"
  (*Enter the Zone*, by Barry Sears)

* "Just eight weeks to a sex-free you!"
  (Okay, I made this one up.)

Y IS FOR YODA, WHO SAID . . .

"Size matters not."
—*Empire Strikes Back*

AUNT AGONY

Dear Aunt Agony,

My friend and I are the same height and bone structure, but he weighs less than I do, even though he exercises less and eats more. Why is that?
—Metabolically Confused

DEAR CONFUSED: Auntie has one word for you: GENETICS.

DEAR AUNTIE,
ALL OF MY JEANS WEAR OUT IN THE VERY SAME PLACE—
BETWEEN MY THIGHS. I'M TIRED OF SPENDING ALL MY MONEY ONLY
TO HAVE PANTS WEAR OUT IN TWO MONTHS. WHAT SHOULD I DO?
—BARE THIGHS

DEAR THIGHS: Auntie has two suggestions: First, leather trousers will not only wear better than cheap cloth, they'll _feel_ better, too (_Ooh, leather_!). Second, try spending more time engaged in activities that don't require your thighs to meet.

dear aunt agony,

how can I learn to forget about my body during sex and just enjoy it?
—anxious when naked

DEAR ANXIOUS: _Forget_ about your body? My poor, anxious dear, sex is _about_ your body. Learn to love it!

DEAR AUNTIE,

PEOPLE ARE AFRAID TO NAG ME TO LOSE WEIGHT. BUT WHEN I'M IN A GROUP OF PEOPLE, THEY TALK ABOUT DIETING TO EACH OTHER. SHOULD I IGNORE IT OR WHAT?
—SCARY FAT PERSON

DEAR AWE-INSPIRING FAT PERSON! Good! Keep doing whatever it is that has them awed! If they're afraid of you, they aren't going to bother you with insults, etc. Now, to carry it to the next level, you must learn to annoy them. Talk constantly about anti-diet philosophy. Regale them with the horrors of weight-loss surgery, the dangers of diet pills. Converse endlessly about how gorgeous your fat friends are. Try it! It's easy and fun.

DEAR AUNT AGONY,

I'm sure that my boyfriend is attracted to me, but he doesn't want to be seen in public with me because I'm fat. What should I do? I feel like a
—SOCIAL PARIAH

DEAR SOCIAL: Are you dirty? Do you smell? Pick your nose in public? Belch at the table? No? Then your boyfriend is obviously insecure, if the opinions of strangers on the street matter to him. First ask yourself: Do you really want to be with someone who is that easily intimidated? If not, then dump the turkey. However, if you think there's still hope for your boyfriend, follow these tactics:

1. Enroll him in an assertiveness training course. It may help him stand up to rude comments from strangers with bigger mouths than brains.

2. Go out without him. Then come back and tell him what fun you've had. He'll feel left out and a fool (which, of course, would be true).

3. Explain to your boyfriend about fat pride, and if he doesn't get it, try Aunt Agony's first suggestion: Dump the turkey. You (in fact, all of us) deserve better treatment than what you've described.

YOU, TOO, CAN BE FLABULOUS!

WHILE AGO, I STARTED SIGNING THE BOTTOM of my correspondence with the salutation, "Stay flabulous!" It makes me giggle every time I write it, with a kind of giddy, rebellious glee. The more I use the word, the more flabulous I feel.

To me, flabulous is exactly the attitude that *FAT!SO?* celebrates. *Flabulous* means not apologizing for your size. It means laughing at your detractors because you really do find them silly. Feeling flabulous means having that special something that makes people wish they had whatever it is you've got. True flabulousness is not exclusive—it inspires others, invites others, sometimes even compels others to explore their *own* flabulous streak. There's plenty to go around. I can't tell you where flabulous comes from or exactly how it will happen for you. All I can say is that waiting for someone else to give you permission is the opposite of flabulous. So is relying on someone else's step-by-step directions. You are the authority here, and only you can make sure that you stay flabulous.

Nonetheless, it doesn't hurt to surround yourself with as much flabulousness as possible. When people started reading my sign-off, they responded with their own definitions of flabulous. I was thrilled that my use of the word prompted other flabulous folk to elaborate on the idea. Here's how the word is spreading.

Martha Mestl writes, "Flabulous means we are all beautiful, exciting, fantastic, wonderful, fabulous, fat people."

Mary McGill answers, "On top of that fact, we actually, really are allowed to feel that way, *and* we have the right to proclaim our flabulousness to the whole wide world."

Haley Hertz says, "Flabulous means never having to say you're saggy!"

And Mike Gorman adds that, besides being an obvious combination of *flab* and *fabulous*, both great words, staying flabulous means a variety of things to him:

✳ "It means I don't have to weigh my meals on a tiny scale, or weigh *myself* on one, either."

✳ "It means standing up strong against the constant stream of fat-negative everything that our culture throws at us."

✳ "It means not being afraid to eat or just let it all

HUG A FAT PERSON. IF YOU'VE NEVER TRIED IT, YOU'LL DEFINITELY LIKE IT.

hang out when I go home to visit my family."

* "It means being truly in love with every square inch of my body, like loving the feel of my hand on my full belly after a particularly good meal."

* "It means not being afraid to tell my boss that an XL or XXL staff shirt will not do for this summer. (It took a lot, and I don't know why, to tell her that if she couldn't get me at least a 3X not to bother because I wouldn't wear it. Sigh of relief. My silly worrying was for naught. They simply got me a shirt that fit.)"

* "And finally . . . it means to be free!"

Whatever it means to you, here is my sincere wish that you find your own way to . . . Stay flabulous!

Z IS FOR HUZZAH!

"There will come a time when you won't even be ashamed if you are fat."

—Frank Zappa, in the song, "Take Your Clothes off when You Dance."

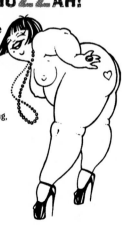

SHELF LIFE

SOME THINGS, JUST BY SITTING SOMEWHERE *on a shelf in your house, help make life worth living. They have shelf life. I don't mean to sound like the ultimate consumer. I just want to share some of the books and publications and films and songs that have supported my flabulous fatso lifestyle—because there's enough stuff out there designed to make you feel bad. This stuff will make you feel good: good and angry, good about yourself, and ready for the good life.*

* **The Afterlife Diet** by Daniel Pinkwater. It's the ultimate fat novel. I've said it before, and I'll say it again. Buy this hilarious book. Buy it for the vampire parakeets, for the fat sex scene, or for the joyous skewering of all manner of weight-loss shysters. Just buy it! It'll remind you why they call it a belly laugh. After you devour *Diet*, Mr. Pinkwater's smorgasbord of tasty children's books awaits you, most notably, the new Larry series, with art by the incomparable Jill Pinkwater.

* **Airline Seating Guide.** This reference book lists which seats have extra leg or hip room

TAKE A SELF-DEFENSE CLASS. ASK THE INSTRUCTOR ABOUT WAYS TO USE YOUR WEIGHT TO YOUR ADVANTAGE.

on domestic flights. It actually gives the measurement in inches of each seat on each kind of plane. If you're fated to sit in seat 17B on a 737, you'll know exactly what you are (or are not) getting into. Tell your travel agent to buy a copy of this slightly pricey volume, and you'll be doing your fellow travelers (wide or tall) a big favor. Available from Carlson Publishing, P.O. Box 888, Los Alamitos, California 90720.

* **Aunty Pua's Dilemma.** Written and illustrated by Ann Kondo Corum. My dear friends Matt and Geoff brought this children's book back

that pigs were meant to be FAT? Accept that fact and WEAR your hat." Aunty Pua buys a colorful muumuu and parties with all the other pigs. Great drawings, plus you learn Hawaiian words for belly (*opu*), buttocks (*'okole*), large (*momona*), coconut pudding (*haupia*), unconditional love (*aloha*), and more. There are even traditional recipes in the back. Call Native Books at (800) 887-7751.

* **Biker Billy Cooks with Fire.** Get this inspiring book, based on Bill Huffnagle's excellent cable-acess TV show of the same name. Biker Billy calls himself a fat man with a frying pan.

CALORIES IN A FIG NEWTON: 50
CALORIES IN A REDUCED-FAT FIG NEWTON: 70

from Hawaii. It begins, "Aunty Pua, that portly pig, has a dilemma that's very big." Yep, she's gained weight lately and has nothing to wear to the party. Various reducing attempts ensue, including a hilarious scene with Pua'a Wiwi (Skinny Pig), a Richard Simmons lookalike swine. Finally, she consults wise Uncle Akamai, M.D., who says, "Aunty Pua, Aunty Pua, you silly pig! You're running and running, and still you're so BIG! Don't you know

He rides a 1996 Harley police motorcycle and lives by the motto, "Eat hot. Ride safe, and cook with fire." Call (800) BIKER-BILLY or write to P.O. Box 124, Florham Park, New Jersey, 17932, to find out whether the show airs in your area.

* **Chef** from Comedy Central's *South Park* cartoon. All Chef can cook is Salisbury steak, but for a good time, *and* a good laugh, you can count on this animated construction-paper character. He'll make sweet love to you all

night long. If none of your friends have boot-leg videos, just get some Isaac Hayes CDs and animate your own evening.

* **Fat Chance.** Fat guy Rick Zakowich's brilliant movie about how he stopped dieting. It won the Canadian equivalent of an Oscar for best documentary. You'll plotz over the cow scene. Get the video from Bullfrog Films, P.O. Box 149, Oley, Pennsylvania 19547; (800) 543-3764.

* **FaT GiRL: The Zine for Fat Dykes and the Women Who Want Them.** "But I like it, too!" I say. And so will you. *FaT GiRL* has steamy stories, great roundtable discussions on tough topics, interviews with famous women, lists of cool resources, comics and photos and rants, and more. It's just so moist! Write to 2215-R Market Street #197, San Francisco, California 94114.

* **Fat Lip Readers Theatre.** This fifteen-year-old troupe of sassy fat women confronts stereotypes in sketches, stories, songs, and skits in the best tradition of in-your-face spoken word. Get the video from P.O. Box 29963, Oakland, California 94604. Or better yet, see them live in one of their San Francisco/Bay Area performances.

* **FAT!SO?.** If you like the book, you'll love the zine. Each issue is packed with new Anatomy Lesson photos, cut 'n' paste projects, sassy comebacks, advice from Aunt Agony, personal tales of wit and woe, and much more. Call (800) OH-FATSO or write to FAT!SO? at P.O. Box 423464, San Francisco, California 94142.

* **Kobuta no Pippo** (a pig called Pippo) by Sanrio, the folks who brought us Hello Kitty. Get the Pippo cartoon character wallet, the rubber stamps, the pencil case, the locking diary, and above all, get the barrettes. This fat little piggy has gotten me through some pretty rough times. Call Sanrio for your very own catalog: (800) 2-SANRIO.

* **NAAFA (the National Association to Advance Fat Acceptance).** Get the newsletter, the NAAFA workbook, and all the cool stuff from the book service. But NAAFA is so much more than that. It's parties and dances and fashion shows and conventions where you'll have the time of your life. It's fat community. It's a sane haven in a thin-crazy world. It's a group with a thirty-year tradition of making life better for fat people, and you're invited to join in. Call (800) 442-1214, or write to NAAFA, P.O. Box 188620, Sacramento, California 95818.

* **"New Chub-ette."** A song by The Crabs. The lyrics go, "Go to school. She's cute, you bet! Got a thing for the new chub-ette. ... She's got

MAKE YOUR OWN FAT-POSITIVE ART. IT'S FUN TO DRAW OR SCULPT VOLUMINOUS, ROUND SHAPES.

a brain and a heart so big, needs a body to hold them in. Get a fry and a shake to go. Won't back down to the status quo . . . Two times two and two times four. Two-time her, and she's out the door." The song is on the *Periscope* CD/LP compilation from Yoyo Recordings. Write to P. O. Box 2462, Olympia, Washington, 98507, or order it online at www.olywa.net/yoyo.

* *Shadow on a Tightrope: Writings by Women on Fat Oppression.* Edited by Lisa Schoenfielder and Barb Wieser. This book changed my life. Because of it, I joined NAAFA and saw Fat Lip Readers Theatre and wrote for *Radiance* and then started *FAT!SO?*, which led me to write this book. Available from Aunt Lute Books, P.O. Box 410687, San Francisco, California 94941.

* *Size Wise: A Catalog of More Than 1,000 Resources for Living with Confidence and Comfort at Any Size,* by Judy Sullivan. This book is like having your own personalized Yellow Pages of every single cool, fat-related thing there is. I don't know how I ever lived without it. Separate chapters cover clothing, health care, exercise equipment and classes

and videos, public accommodations, social groups and dating services nationwide, fat activist groups, all-important stuff for fat kids, fat-positive music and movies and TV shows and books and magazines and Web sites, and more. *Size Wise* came out from Avon Books in 1997.

* *Cooking with the Two Fat Ladies,* by Jennifer Paterson and Clarissa Dickson Wright, is the cookbook that accompanies the most wonderful cooking show of all time. It airs on the Food Channel, but you can also get an idea of Jennifer and Clarissa's delicious forthrightness from this book. For example, Clarissa was asked whether she didn't find the title of the series, *Two Fat Ladies*, rather offensive. She replied, "We don't mind 'Two,' and there's nothing wrong with 'Fat,' but we don't like 'Ladies.' It makes us sound like a public convenience." Oh, did I mention that the stars, Jennifer and Clarissa, ride around the English countryside in their vintage Triumph motorbike with sidecar? Also, who can resist recipes like Raised Tongue Pie, Mustard Bloaters, Bacon Cake, or Haggis Waldorf?

WEAR SOMETHING SPANDEX, THE BETTER TO ADMIRE YOUR OWN LUSCIOUS CURVES.

FAT!SO? TRADING CARDS!
THE HEROES & VILLAINS OF FAT HISTORY

HERO

GANESHA
HINDU DEITY

VILLAIN

JEAN NIDETCH
WEIGHT WATCHER

VILLAIN

LOUIS DUBLIN
INSURANCE EXEC

HERO

LILLIAN RUSSELL
SINGER

JEAN NIDETCH
WEIGHT WATCHER

VILLAINY: She turned dieting into an industry.

BROCHURE-SPEAK: "It began in 1961, when Jean found a diet she could live with and lost 72 pounds. She wanted to share her success [sic] with others and invited six overweight [sic] friends [sic] to meet with her in her Queens, N.Y. apartment."

BAD GUYS FINISH FIRST: Her autobiography sold over 2 million copies. *Ladies Home Journal* called her "One of The Most Important Women in the U.S." *London Sunday Times* said, "One of the 1,000 makers of the 20th century." And she was the Horatio Alger Association's outstanding American for 1989.

HORTICULTURE: In 1992, she christened the Weight Watcher tulip. There's the "Jean Nidetch Rose," too.

THE TOLL: 25 million Weight Watchers worldwide.

BLOOD MONEY: She founded the Jean Nidetch Women's Center at the University of Nevada, Las Vegas, where, among other stuff, there's a Food Resource Center and workshops on eating disorders.

GANESHA
HINDU DEITY

OTHER NAMES: Ekadanta, Lambodara, Vakratunda, Vighneshwara, Vinayaka.

SLOGAN: God of wisdom and obstacles

HEROISM: Most lovable of the fat, four-armed gods

PARENTS: The god Shiva and the goddess Parvati

ONE ACCOUNT OF HIS BIRTH: Shiva liked to disturb Parvati during her bath, so she formed Ganesha from her bath scrapings and had him guard the door. Shiva ripped Ganesha's head off. Parvati, miffed, sent Shiva to find a replacement. The first noggin he came across was that of an elephant.

WEIGHT: "He has swallowed and holds in his vast belly . . . eggs of all the universes and the orbs of destruction (Rudras) by the million and feasted on all the pervaders (Vishnus)."—P.C. Mukherjee, *Report on the Antiquities of the District of Lalitput*

HOBBIES: Dancing, eating sweetmeats and turmeric

HANGOUTS: Doorways, parades, buffet lines

CONVEYANCE: A rat

LILLIAN RUSSELL
SINGER

REAL NAME: Helen Louise Leonard

CAREER CHOICE: Sex symbol and Broadway star

REIGN: 1861–1922

WEIGHT: 165–200 pounds

HEROISM: For her day, Lillian was fatter, sexier, and more famous than Madonna. And just as rich.

HUSBANDS AND COMPANIONS: Harry Braham (1879), Edward Solomon (1883), Signor Giovanni Perugini (1894), and Jesse Lewiohn (1896)

BEST FRIENDS: Diamond Jim Brady, Marie Dressler

PASSIONS: Poker, horses, jewels, the stage, and food

EXERCISE: Riding her gold-plated bicycle

SALARY: $35,000 in 1890, $119,000 in 1891

HORTICULTURE: The American Beauty Rose was named after Lillian Russell.

TELECOMMUNICATIONS: She made the first long-distance call, to President Grover Cleveland.

MUSIC: In her prime, she hit high C eight times during each performance. (Try that, Madonna!)

LOUIS DUBLIN
INSURANCE EXEC

EMPLOYER: Metropolitan Life Insurance Co.

TITLE: Third Vice President and Statistician

VILLAINY: Created and popularized height/weight charts.

LIFE EXPECTANCY: 1882–1969

THE BIG LIE: "At all adult ages now, underweight may be conducive to long life." —Dublin, 1949

BOOKS BY DUBLIN: *The Excesses of Birth Control* (1925), *The Money Value of a Man* (1947)

MAD SCIENTIST INVENTION: Dublin invented the concept of frame size for his height/weight charts (thereby narrowing the "ideal" weight range from about 30 pounds to about 10 pounds) despite the fact that his source data did not specify frame size.

LEGACY: In 1931, thanks to his charts, more people were denied life insurance for "overweight" than for any other reason. (Of the 9 percent denied insurance, 3 percent were fat. Only 1.25 percent were denied for heart disease.) Fat folk are still routinely denied insurance based on Dublin's pioneering work.

FAT!SO? TRADING CARDS!
THE HEROES & VILLAINS OF FAT HISTORY

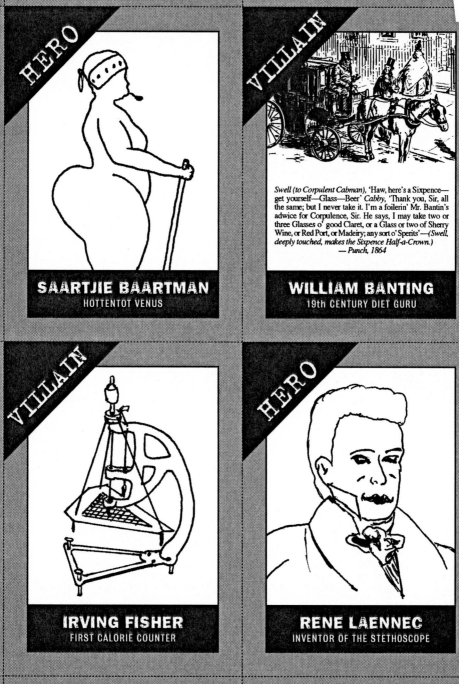

HERO

SAARTJIE BAARTMAN
HOTTENTOT VENUS

VILLAIN

Swell (to Corpulent Cabman), 'Haw, here's a Sixpence—get yourself—Glass—Beer' *Cabby,* 'Thank you, Sir, all the same; but I never take it. I'm a foilerin' Mr. Bantin's adwice for Corpulence, Sir. He says, I may take two or three Glasses o' good Claret, or a Glass or two of Sherry Wine, or Red Port, or Madeiry; any sort o' Sperits'—*(Swell, deeply touched, makes the Sixpence Half-a-Crown.)*
— *Punch, 1864*

WILLIAM BANTING
19th CENTURY DIET GURU

VILLAIN

IRVING FISHER
FIRST CALORIE COUNTER

HERO

RENE LAENNEC
INVENTOR OF THE STETHOSCOPE

WILLIAM BANTING
19th CENTURY DIET GURU

VILLAINY: Wrote the first popular modern diet book
BEST-SELLER: *Letter on Corpulence*, 1863
NEOLOGISMS: Banting (dieting); to bant (to diet)
SALES: More than 58,000 copies at a sixpence apiece
HIS LOSS: 46 pounds in one year (from 202 to 156)
WHY BANT? He had "an inexpressible dread of such a calamity [fat]," had to take stairs backwards, couldn't tie his shoes, "nor attend to the little offices humanity requires without considerable pain and difficulty," suffered loss of hearing, and boils.
HIS DIAGNOSIS IN HINDSIGHT: adult-onset diabetes
THE BANTING METHOD: Meat, green vegetables, toast, alcohol. No "starches" or "sacharinoids."
IMITATORS: The Scarsdale diet, *Calories Don't Count*
FORMULA: The Before Photo: "I deeply regret not having secured a photographic portrait of myself in 1862, to place in juxtaposition with one of my present form." He also gave us these classics: ask-a-doctor, try-it-a-month, you-won't-be-hungry, I-did-it-so-can-you.

SAARTJIE BAARTMAN
HOTTENTOT VENUS

HERITAGE: Bushman, Griqua, Hottentot, or !Kung
1810: A doctor took her from South Africa to London, where she was caged nude, displayed in public.
1815: A prostitute in France, she died at age 27.
EURO VIEW: The propriety of her exhibition was tried in court. Scientists examined her large buttocks and vulva, and wrote (self-defeating) articles, using her to prove white superiority. After her death, her skeleton, brain, and genitalia were kept on display in Paris' *Musée de l'Homme* (Museum of Man) until the 1970s.
ENCORE(?): Since then, the museum has displayed her remains *again*, as part of an exhibit on 19th century racism toward aboriginal people.
DÉJÀ-VU: Today, South Africa's Griqua claim Saartjie as an ancestor, a symbol in their effort to reclaim their tribal lands. The French refuse to return her remains. Meanwhile, another tribe, the San (or Bushmen), live as "virtual tourist exhibits at a game reserve in the Northern Cape province," says the *San Francisco Chronicle*.

RENE LAENNEC
INVENTOR OF THE STETHOSCOPE

BEST-SELLER: *Traité de l'Ausculation Médiate*, 1819
PRICE OF THE FIRST STETHOSCOPE: Three francs
HOW IT HAPPENED: "In 1816 I was consulted by a young woman. Owing to her stoutness little information could be gathered by application of the hand and percussion. The patient's age and sex did not permit me to resort to the kind of examination I have just described (i.e., direct application of the ear to the chest). I recalled a well-known acoustic phenomenon: namely, if you place your ear against one end of a wooden beam the scratch of a pin at the other extremity is most distinctly audible. It occured to me that this physical property might serve a useful purpose in this case. Taking a sheaf of paper I rolled it into a very tight roll. . . I was both surprised and gratified at being able to hear the beating of the heart with much greater clearness and distinctness than I had ever done before."
MORAL: The wise physician respects the fat patient.

IRVING FISHER
FIRST CALORIE COUNTER

CREDENTIALS: Yale University economist
VILLAINY: Invented the 100-calorie portion in 1906
VILLAINY W/FUDGE SAUCE: Used WWI rationing, poverty, and the Depression to popularize calorie counting.
BEST-SELLER: *How to Live* (1920s)
SALES: 500,000 copies in 18 editions
FOUNDER: Life Extension Institute
MAD SCIENTIST INVENTION: The Mechanical Diet Indicator (*obverse*) required one to locate on a chart the protein, fat, and carbo content of the 100-calorie portions of food one ate; plot them on a triangular grid; and locate the cumulative point in the device. A tilting triangle indicated diet "imbalance."
450-CALORIE PIE SLICE IN THE SKY: "One soon becomes able to recognize the quantities of ordinary foods which contain 100 calories, and to hold in memory their position on the triangle. Very little thought will then enable him to judge . . . whether their centre of gravity falls within the rectangle indicated."

SUSANNA COCROFT
WWI-ERA DIET GURU

VILLAINY: Was the Susan Powter of her generation.

RÉSUMÉ: (*Note Cocroft's eery similarities to Powter*)

1902: Sells mail-order booklets on diet, exercise, posture, and positive thinking. Early infomercials.

1918: Writes best-seller, *The Woman Worth While*

1918: Hired by War Dept. to get women workers healthy. Starts callisthenics camp. Endorsed by Surgeon General.

1919: Claims 600,000 women requested diet help

1920: Claims to have reduced 40,000 of them

POWTERISMS: Cocroft's slogan: "Be happy. *Enjoy* life. You can weigh exactly what you *should*."

THOUGHTS ON INTERIOR DECOR: "A woman overburdened with flesh, untidy in outline, suggesting physical overindulgence, in a neat, tidy, attractive, artistic home is like a cheap chromo in an expensive handwrought frame."

SOURCE: Hillel Schwartz's brilliant book, *Never Satisfied: A Cultural History of Diets and Fat.*

AMALIE MATERNA
WAGNERIAN SOPRANO

HEROISM: Created the Fat Lady icon in opera

1867: Premiered the role of Brünnhilde at Wagner's opera house in Bayreuth, Germany

1887: Premiered the role again at the Met in New York

1978: San Antonio sportscaster Daniel John Cook popularized the phrase, "The opera ain't over 'til the fat lady sings."

HER SISTER BRÜNNHILDES: the round and renowned Kirsten Flagstad, Olive Fremstad, Johanna Gadski, Margaret Harshaw, Marjorie Lawrence, Lili Lehmann, Margarete Matzenauer, Lillian Nordica, Eugenie Pappenheim (the first American Brünnhilde), Milka Ternina, Helen Traubel, Cyrena Van Gordon

LUISA TETRAZZINI: A fat coloratura *so* gifted she didn't need lessons to become an opera star at Covent Garden in 1907 *or* to inspire the dish, Chicken Tetrazzini.

MARIETTA ALBONI: Mozart's favorite soprano, her weight made opera-length standing uncomfortable, so she performed sitting down—to rave reviews.

RICHARD A. JEWELL
FORMER SECURITY GUARD

HEROISM: Saved hundreds of lives during the Olympics when he spotted a suspicious knapsack and alerted police, who found a bomb in it.

HEROISM: Despite the risk to his life, the security guard stayed on duty, going back inside a tower to clear people from the danger area below. (Two people died and 100 were injured when the bomb went off.)

HEROISM: Endured three months of constant media hounding and an FBI investigation while he was wrongly accused of planting the bomb.

HEROISM: Endured rude comments about his size from national media, who called him, "bulky" (*Time*), "portly" (*Reuters*), "The Unabubba," "hefty," "chunky," "beefy," "blubberguts," "poor slob," "fat loser," and "pudgy nobody." (This last from a hatchet piece by Mike Royko, who wrote, "Without prejudging him [hah!—*ed.*], it would be easy to put together a scenario in which someone like Jewell does something that *normal* [emphasis added] people would consider unthinkable.)

HEROISM: Carried himself with dignity through it all.

C. EVERETT KOOP
FORMER U. S. SURGEON GENERAL

VILLAINY: Declared war on fat (and fatsoes) December 6, 1994, in a press conference at the White House rose garden.

VILLAINY: Koop acts like he's the nation's selfless old pediatrician, but he's paid by the diet industry.

VILLAINY: Claimed that fat-related diseases cost the U.S. $100 billion a year. That number includes all spending on weight loss products, even diet Coke. Diet drinks are a fat-related disease? Jenny Craig is a sickness? (Of a sort.) Oh, any fat person who ever got sick, that counts too.

VILLAINY: In a speech, he said, "Doctors aren't talking to their patients enough about obesity. They need to tell their patients, 'Hey, you've got to get the lard [*sic*] off.'"

VILLAINY: Koop and wife bought a multi-story house to get more exercise and lose weight. Only got one phone, so they'd use the stairs more. (Koop was 80, by the way.) He had reconstructive knee surgery recently. Too much stair climbing, hm? Does that count as fat-related disease or just plain stupidity?

CONTRIBUTORS

Mercedes Abraham is an artist and writer living in San Francisco with her son and her two canaries. She's also living comfortably in an ever-changing body.

Kathy Barron is 34, mother of a six-year-old daughter, divorced, a massage therapist, and a happy, free human being.

Jeff Beeson is a twenty-six-year-old mechanic who lives in the San Francisco Bay Area. He enjoys working on and racing his '69 Dodge Charger. He's a cute, hairy fat guy, who can be reached by e-mail at jbeeson@slip.net.

Porter Bennefield is a retired air force technical sergeant and a published poet. He is currently pursuing a degree in journalism at a local college. He has traveled throughout the world and enjoys spending time on the California coast.

Alan Blalock is a white-collar (though he never wears a white shirt nor a tie) paper pusher who wishes he was a mechanic. He lives in San Jose, California, with too many cars and not enough garage space. He also shares space with the typical suburban (yeah, he has one of those too) animals—two dogs, a cat, and a goldfish—three offspring (children), and a wife.

Johanne Blank, poster child for the United Perverts College Fund, is living proof of what happens when you send someone with a dirty mind to graduate school. An unapologetically fat, opinionated, Jewish loudmouth sexpot, she writes the "Sexpot Savant" column for the *Boston Phoenix*, publishes erotica and sex-related nonfiction regularly, and is writing her dissertation, entitled "Witches, Bitches, Whores, and Britches," on mezzosopranos. She lives near Boston and relishes notoriety.

Boanne is a fat, forty-year-old mother/homemaker in early retirement, which means she pretty much does whatever she wants, whenever she wants. Her passions are nature, classical music, art, literature, all kinds of needlework, reading, writing, computers, the internet, and learning everything possible before leaving the planet. She can be reached by e-mail at boanne@sound.net.

Randi Cecchine is a photographer and videomaker, and works with Paper Tiger Television (www.papertiger.org), a nonprofit video collective that has been "smashing the myths of the information industry" since 1981.

Geoffrey Dryvynsyde is a lawyer and law school teacher who lives in San Francisco. His practice focuses on the social problems caused by large corporate entities that wield extensive power. He enjoys drinking whiskey and has been known to defeat Marilyn Wann at backgammon.

Betty Rose Dudley is a fat working-class dyke from Missouri who now lives, works, writes, and plays in the San Francisco Bay Area. Her piece, "Fat Kills," has been reprinted in many books and publications, including *Utne Reader* and the 1996 *Women Writers* calendar.

When she isn't praying for rain, **Kristine Durden** is a college-radio DJ, a 'zine editor, a ukulele player/songwriter, and a store manager of Says Who?, a large-size clothing store for women. She can be reached by e-mail at karaw@kzsu.stanford.edu.

Dawn Falkowich is sixteen years old and has ultra-magenta hair. She hopes people can have a better outlook about themselves and life in general, because depressing people are no fun. Remember: Don't let any-

195

one judge you; if you're okay with who you are, that's all that really matters.

Yalith Fonfa is fourteen years old and lives in New York City. She came out as a lesbian at twelve and a half and as a fatso the next year. She connects the two issues as being about accepting and loving herself, no matter what societal boundaries she has to break.

Michelle Haegle is a well-rounded traveler who loves to learn about new people, places, and things. She has been big ever since she was little.

Bonnie Hawthorne has a genetic predisposition against bios.

Betsy "Boo" Mitchell Henning prides herself on being too big to fit in pigeonholes. She has ⅛-inch-long magenta hair. She works as the worship coordinator for a nondenominational Christian church and lives near Baltimore with her husband of seven years, Eric. She listens to really loud music all day long, and is pleased to have reached a point in her life where her inside is beginning to match her outside.

Sharon Hendrickson is a thirty-three-year-old budding fat admirer . . . *and* she has a pretty face! Beyond that, she is a warm person with a quick sense of humor, happily married, and was recently the largest law student graduating from Ohio State!

Haley Hertz is a whirling dervish who defies description and hates tooting her own horn. You can read her humor column, "Haley's Comments," in *What's On in Las Vegas* magazine, or online at www.ilovevegas.com.

Lorna Hommel is a government contracting specialist residing in the beautiful state of Maryland, home of the blue crab. She likes collecting seashells and key chains

and enjoys various types of crafts. Other than these boring things, she's lots of fun . . . really!

Joanna Iovino is a Long Island Generation Xer who is proud to be f-a-t fat as well as p-h-a-t phat.

Although many large families tend to develop extreme conformity, in contrast to the immense wealth of her siblings, **Emily Ivie**, *aka* MLEIV, (a six-year college dropout) has become an utter and pathetic failure. This strange twist of fate allows her siblings to belligerently ridicule her philosophies (if she were right, she'd be wealthy, eh?) and also to persecute her publicly at family gatherings.

Debora Iyall is a recording and visual artist with six albums to her credit, including the 1982 Romeo Void dance track hit, "Nvr Say Nvr." Her original prints have been exhibited in galleries and museums. For information about her latest projects, including her new band, Knife in Water, and its new release, *DIALOG*, write to Pan Records, P.O. Box 41-1447, San Francisco, California 94141, or visit Debora's Web site at www.crl.com/~diyall.

Bethany Johnsen lives in Portland, Maine. She enjoys latch hooking rugs and painting.

Jack Keely is a Los Angeles-based cartoonist who has illustrated numerous books, including the popular "Grossology" series.

John Latham is an assistant manager at a plastics company in Louisana. He is a former air traffic controller, and has played guitar for fourteen years.

A collector of fire idols, doggie diner memorabilia, and stories, **Elsa L. T. Lee** photographs the stars, sights, and sounds of San Francisco. Notes, love offerings, and inquiries can be sent to 1001 Page Street, Box 51, San Francisco, California, 94117.

Ole Joergen Malm is a Norwegian man with a rare, 11:19 chromosome translocation. He is a graphic designer and cartoonist.

Donna Marsh plays an astrologer on the Internet. She is about to become a published poet. In the meantime, she bakes, because she just found a treasure trove of old cookbooks.

Lynn McAfee, *aka* **Lynn Mabel-Lois**, was an original member of the radical fat feminist group Fat Underground in 1973. She is now director of medical advocacy for the Council on Size and Weight Discrimination. Much of her time is spent advocating on behalf of fat people, with doctors, researchers, and government agencies. She showers daily, but doesn't lather.

Cynthia Meier happily lives in Tucson, Arizona, with her husband, Tom. She is often an actor and writer but is currently composting, waiting for the next creative seed to sprout.

Susan Miller rang in the new year by putting on her size 6X bathing suit and climbing into a hot tub with a bunch of skinny strangers. As she approaches her forties, she feels a great urgency to rid herself of the things that have been weighing her down, such as shame and fear. Her one resolution this year: Whatever it is I'm doing right now, DO IT. No more eating without tasting, because I'm thinking of sixteen other things I should be doing. Regarding *FAT!SO?*: It is wonderful to be reminded that this business of becoming a human being is not all struggle. There is wit, camaraderie, and sex, too. Knockers up!

Alexis Neptune is a writer, theologian, and artist who is seeking ways to grow comfortable in her Rubenesque shell. Writing on fat and female issues are part of this attempt. Look for her comic book, *Buffy and Jodi's Guide to the Galaxy*. Contact her by e-mail at lex@icanect.net.

Nicole M. Nicholson is a technical support specialist who lives in Columbus, Ohio. She is a 1998 graduate of Bowling Green State University and holds a B.A. in communications. She is currently attached to a wonderful woman and is a rabid fan of R.E.M., George Carlin, and good coffee.

Panda's real name is Claudia Strong. She includes being a lesbian, feminist, animal lover, fat activist, liberal, and an artist as aspects of herself.

Tracy Pekar-Rogers lives in Houston, Texas, and is studying psychology, with the plan of one day becoming a therapist. She is also a jewelry/clothing artist and is active in local size-positive groups. You can e-mail her at auroraeB@aol.com.

Randa Powers is living large in the Midwest, proving the Corn Belt is big enough for anyone. A hard-working baby boomer, Randa enjoys the thrill of auctions and junk shops, amassing a great deal of objets d'art that stir conversation and curiosity—much as she has tried to do her entire life.

Lyn Sheffield is an outrageously flirty, succulent, sensuous sister livin', lovin', and changing many a Washington, D.C., area man's mind about just how desirable a fat woman is.

Ron Sol is a freelance artist and cartoonist in the San Francisco Bay Area.

Sondra Solovay is trying to drive herself out of business. She has always fought for social justice. Since graduating from UC Berkeley's law school, she has worked to end fat discrimination, as a legal consultant specializing in weight-related cases. Her book, *Tipping the Scales of Justice*, is due out in 1999 and will be the first book to thoroughly examine how fat affects courtroom justice. She can be reached at 2625 Alcatraz

Avenue, #261, Berkeley, California 94705, or by e-mail at solo@sirius.com.

Patia Stephens is a journalism student and writer who lives in a homestead cabin in the hills above Missoula, Montana, with her cat, Tango Deluxe. She believes it's possible to change the world, one person at a time.

Kristen Tabbutt-Scheck is a senior in college, majoring in social sciences. She lives in Hubert, North Carolina, and enjoys music, reading, writing poetry, and hanging out at coffee shops.

Patricia Schwarz is a fine arts photographer who has exhibited, published, and had her work collected internationally. She is the recipient of several international photography awards. Her work-in-progress is a series of portrait and nude studies of large women entitled *Women of Substance*. Patricia is available to give slide presentations. Contact her at P.O. Box 8084, Berkeley, California 94707-8084.

Carol Squires is a photographer by training, a fat woman by genetics (and years of dieting), and a fat activist by necessity for her own survival. A member of Fat Lip Readers Theatre for twelve years, she lives and loves in the San Francisco Bay Area.

Cath Thompson is a fat, polyamorous, kinky dyke living in San Francisco. She channels Aunt Agony with alarming regularity. While Cath may not always follow Auntie's excellent advice, you should. Cath can be reached by e-mail at qtfatgirl@aol.com. Questions for Auntie should be addressed to auntie@fatso.com.

Heather Urban is an amateur doodler currently residing in San Francisco's East Bay with her four large cats and schnooky.

Charles Van Dyke is forty-eight years old. He lives with his wife Katharine and their cats in El Monte, California. Charles first joined NAAFA in the seventies, and has worked for the organization in various roles ever since. In 1995, Charles shared his life story for a *Gentlemen's Quarterly* article called, "Big—America's War Against Fatties." Charles has his own consulting business and is a part-time yoga teacher. His current interests include panning for gold, computers and the Internet, science fiction, and Jyotish (Vedic astrology).

Yuri Vann is an artist who lives in Lansing, Michigan. He believes that making women insecure about their bodies is the method society uses to control them. He wants his art to show his love for the everyday, working class woman.

NOTES

Pages 7–207: Flip book art by Ron Sol, with acknowledgment to the work of Preston Blair and Tex Avery.

Page 10: Dieters and states' population figures come from the Calorie Control Council and the 1990 census. These fun fat facts were researched by Sondra Solovay.

Page 13: Fat cell photo from Donald W. Fawcett, M.D., Hersey Professor of Anatomy and Cell Biology, Emeritus, Harvard Medical School.

Page 20: Art by Ron Sol.

Page 22: Butt photos by Debora Iyall.

Page 26: Sydney photo by Geoffrey Dryvynsyde.

Page 27: Italy photo by Laura Fraser; New York City photo by Randi Cecchine; Paris photos by Geoffrey Dryvynsyde; New Orleans and San Francisco photos by Marilyn Wann.

Page 30: Jogger rubber stamp by Jeanne Borofsky. Rubber Stamps of America, P. O. Box 567, Saxtons River, Vermont 05154.

Pages 32–33: Life-span data for smokers and people who eat low-fat diets come from Warren S. Browner, "What if Americans Ate Less Fat? A Quantitative Estimate of the Effect on Mortality," *Journal of the American Medical Association* 265, no. 24 (June 1991): 3285–3291. This fun fact was researched by Sondra Solovay.

Page 34: Art by Mercedes Abraham.

Pages 35–36: Kevin R. Fontaine, et al., "Body Weight and Health Care Among in the General Population," *Archives of Family Medicine*, volume 7, July/August 1998.

Page 36: David R. Williams, et al., "Discrimination, Race, and Health," a paper presented at the 1997 Joint Meeting of the Public Health Conference on Records and Statistics and Data User's Conference, Washington, D.C., July 28–31, 1997. Jerome Kassirer, M.D., and Marcia Angell, M.D., "Losing Weight—An Ill-Fated New Year's Resolution," *New England Journal of Medicine* 338, no.1 (January 1, 1998): 52–54. The definition of starvation comes from the World Health Organization.

Page 37: Risks of dieting come from medical literature researched by Dawn Atkins of the Santa Cruz Body Image Task Force and from Frances M. Berg, *Health Risks of Weight Loss* (Hettinger, North Dakota: *Healthy Weight Journal*, 1992). Findings related to the use of Redux and Fen/Phen come from the National Institutes of Health.

Page 38: Fat data come from June Stevens, et al., "The Effect of Age on the Association between Body Mass and Mortality," *New England Journal of Medicine* 338, no.1 (January 1998). Smoking data comes from "Cigarette Smoking—Attributable Mortality and Years of Potential Life Lost—United States 1990," *Morbidity and Mortality Weekly Report* 42, no. 33 (August 1993): 645–648. Motorcycle data comes from the U.S. Department of Transportation's National Highway Traffic Safety Facts 1996," page 2. Pollution data comes from D. Dockery, et al., "An Association between Air Pollution and Mortality in Six U.S. Cities," *New England Journal of Medicine* 329, no.24 (December, 1993) 1753–1759.

Pages 38–39: Glenn A. Gaesser, Ph.D., *Big Fat Lies: The Truth About Your Weight and Your Health* (New York: Fawcett Columbine, 1996).

Pages 39–40: On fatness and fitness, see Steven Blair, et al., "Physical Fitness, Mortality and Obesity," *International Journal of Obesity* 19, no. 4 (1995): S41–S44.

Page 40: On the health benefits of eccentricity, see David Weeks and Jamie James, *Eccentrics: A Study of Sanity and Strangeness* (New York: Villard, 1995). On the failure of dieting, see F. Kramer, et al., "Long-Term Follow-up of Behavioral Treatment for Obesity: Patterns of Weight Regain Among Men and Women," *International Journal of Obesity* 13, no. 2 (1989): 123–126. On the 784-member National Weight Control Registry, see Rena Wing, et al., "A Descriptive Study of Individuals Successful at Long-Term Mainten-ance of Substantial Weight Loss," *American Journal of Clinical Nutrition* 66, no. 2 (August 1997) 239–246.

Page 41: Cancer risk and and weight-loss probability data come from the Centers for Disease Control and from the NIH Technology Assessment Conference on Methods for Voluntary Weight Loss and Control, 1992.

Page 44: Jerome Kassirer, M.D., and Marcia Angell, M.D., "Losing Weight—An Ill-Fated New Year's Resolution," *New England Journal of Medicine* 338, no.1 (January 1, 1998): 52–54.

Page 46: "Jumping Guy" by Ken Brown for Rubber Stamps of America, P. O. Box 567, Saxtons River, Vermont 05154.

Page 47: Fat power fist art by Yuri Vann.

Pages 47–48: On lefties dying nine years earlier than right-handed people, see Sam Coren, et al., "Left-hand-edness and Life Expectancy," *New England Journal of Medicine* 325, no. 14 (1991): 1041. Nancy Shute, "Life for Lefties: From Annoying to Downright Risky," *Smithsonian* (December 1994).

Page 51: Treblinka information comes from Naomi Wolf, *The Beauty Myth: How Images of Beauty Are Used Against Women* (New York: William Morrow, 1991):195.

Page 52: Big-boned cartoon by Marilyn Wann. Ancel Keys, *Nutrition Review* (1980), as quoted in Glenn A. Gaesser, P.h.D., *Big Fat Lies: The Truth About Your Weight and Your Health* (New York: Fawcett Columbine, 1996).

Page 54: Art by Yuri Vann.

Page 57: Rates of inactivity come from the Department of Health and Human Services and Centers for Disease Control, *The Surgeon General's Report on Physical Activity and Health* (Washington D.C.: GPO, 1996).

Page 58: Model, Chupoo Alafonte; photo, Marilyn Wann.

Page 59: Personals ad research comes from St. Edwards University in Austin, Texas, as reported in *Texas Monthly*, January 1997.

Page 60: Steven Blair, et al.,"Physical Fitness, Mortality and Obesity," *International Journal of Obesity* 19, no. 4 (1995) S41–S44.

Page 61: Photo by Vince Agor.

Page 66: Belly photos by Debora Iyall.

TELL YOUR OWN FAT STORY. WRITE IT DOWN AND SUBMIT IT TO *FAT!SO?* THE ZINE.

Page 68: Estimate of disordered eating among women comes from a clinician who runs an eating disorders clinic, as quoted in Janet Polivy and C. Peter Herman, "Diagnosis and Treatment of Normal Eating," *Journal of Consulting and Clinical Psychology* 5, no.1 (1987).

Page 69–73: Great information about prescription weight-loss drugs comes from Laura Fraser, *Losing It: False Hopes and Fat Profits in the Diet Industry* (New York: Dutton, 1997); Paul Ernsberger and Paul Haskew, "Rethinking Obesity: An Alternative View of Its Health Implications," *The Journal of Obesity and Weight Regulation* 6, no. 2 (summer 1987); and Hillel Schwartz, *Never Satisfied: A Cultural History of Diets, Fantasies, and Fat* (New York: Macmillan, 1996).

Page 75: Puritan vilification of spice is recounted in Michelle Stacey, *Consumed: Why Americans Love, Hate, and Fear Food* (New York: Simon & Schuster, 1994) 199.

Page 76: Orgasm survey comes from *Weight Watchers* magazine, 1996.

Page 78: Stephen Jay Gould, *The Mismeasure of Man* (New York: W.W. Norton, 1996): 406.

Pages 78–79: A. Peck and D. Vagero, "Adult Body Height, Self-Perceived Health and Mortality in the Swedish Population," *Journal of Epidemiology* 43, no. 4 (December 1989): 380–384. P. Allebeck and C. Bergh, "Height, Body Mass Index, and Mortality: Do Social Factors Explain the Association?" *Public Health* 106, no. 5 (September 1992): 375–382.

Page 79: Albert Stunkard, A. Foch, and Z. Hrubek, "A Twin Study of Human Obesity," *Journal of the American Medical Association* 256, no. 1 (July 1986): 51–54. T. Strandberg, "Inverse Relation Between Height and Cardiovascular Mortality in Men During Thirty-Year Follow-up," *American Journal of Cardiology* 80, no. 3 (August 1997): 349–350.

Page 80: Peter Kilborn, "Health Gap Grows, with Black Americans Trailing Whites, Studies Say," *The New York Times* (26 January 1998). Comparative earnings of fat and thin women come from Steven L. Gortmaker, et al., "Social and Economic Consequences of Overweight in Adolescence and Young Adulthood," *New England Journal of Medicine* 329, no. 14 (September 1993): 1008–1012. This fun fat fact was researched by Sondra Solovay.

Page 82: Data on weight gain comes from the National Institutes of Health, the National Center for Health Statistics, and the Centers for Disease Control. This fun fat fact was researched by Sondra Solovay.

Page 83: Art by Heather Urban.

Page 84: Braitman, Adlin, and Stanton, "Obesity and Caloric Intake: The NHANES I," *Journal of Chronic Diseases*, vol. 18, no. 9: 727-732.

Page 89: Planetary poundage appears in Marilyn Vos Savant, "Ask Marilyn," *Parade*.

Page 90: Bowling ball photo by Jeff Beeson.

Page 92: Marketdata Research, as quoted in Laura Fraser, *Losing It: False Hopes and Fat Profits in the Diet Industry* (New York: Dutton, 1997): 8.

Page 93: The unbearable weightiness of sunlight comes from "Einstein Revealed," a *Nova* episode.

Page 94: "Fingers in Ears" by Ken Brown for Rubber Stamps of America, P. O. Box 567, Saxtons River, Vermont 05154.

Page 96: L. M. Boyd, "Grab Bag," *San Francisco Chronicle*.

Page 102: Population data for African-Americans, gays and lesbians, disabled people, and fat people come from *U.S. Statistical Abstract*; Susan Stryker and Jim Van Buskirk, *Gay by the Bay*; Disability Statistics Center at the University of California at San Francisco Medical School, and the National Institutes of Health.

Page 108: Chin photos by Carol Squires.

Page 110: Slim Down with Jesus information comes from TV's *A Current Affair*. This fun fat fact was researched by Sondra Solovay.

Page 111–112: Many brilliant ideas for fun things to do with a bathroom scale were contributed by Hank's Gab Café patrons Johanne Blank, Haley Hertz, Nicole Light-burn, Annie Miller, Patia Stephens, and Charles Van Dyke.

Page 114: Diet failure rates come from the NIH Technology Assessment Conference on Methods for Voluntary Weight Loss and Control, 1992. Miraculous data comes from the *1994 World Almanac*. This fun fact was researched by Sondra Solovay.

Page 115: Double chin photo by Patricia Schwarz.

Page 116: Rubber stamp art by Jack Keely. Alice in Rubberland, P. O. Box 20833, Seattle, Washington 98102.

Page 118: Dorothea Ross and S. Ross, "Teaching the Child with Leukemia to Cope with Teasing," *Issues in Comprehensive Pediatric Nursing* 7 (1984): 59–66.

Page 123: Art by Mercedes Abraham.

Page 124: Revelations about the mechanics of fat people as bone marrow donors come from a UCLA surgeon who prefers not to be named.

Pages 125–126: BMI sources are listed by line.
Pacific Bell Smart Yellow Pages, 1996 (1,2).
Liposuction cost estimates come from an informal survey of plastic surgery Web sites (3).
20/20 (4).
The Top Ten of Everything (5).
U.S. Department of Education (6).
Gallup Organization (7).
Parade magazine survey of thirty-five to sixty-five year olds (8).
Circulation data for 1992, taken from 1993 *Editor and Publisher International Yearbook* (9).
Circulation data for 1992, taken from *The World Almanac* (10).
Largesse: the Network for Size Esteem (11).
Gallup Organization (12).
Time, 23 September 1996 (13,14).
Calorie Control Council, "Ingredient Spotlight on Olestra: Making a Healthier Chip," *Calorie Control Commentary,* 1996 (15).
J. Langlois, et al., "Weight Change Between Age 50 Years and Old Age is Associated with Risk of Hip Fracture in White Women Aged 67 Years and Older," *Archives of Internal Medicine* 156, no. 9 (May 1996): 989–994 (16, 17).
Family Circle Magazine (18).
Marketdata Enterprises (19).
Eva Szekely, *Never Too Thin* (London: Women's Press, 1989) (20).
Steven L. Gortmaker, et al., "Social and Economic Consequences of Overweight in Adolescence and Young Adulthood," *New England Journal of Medicine* 329, no.14 (September, 1993): 1008–1012 (21, 22).
U.S. Census, 1990 (23).
Gina Kolata, "Obesity: A Heavy Burden to Bear," *New York Times,* 22 November 1992 (24).

HIRE A FAT PERSON.

E! News Extra (25).

Data for 1992, from the U.S. Department of Labor's Bureau of Labor Statistics (26).

Estimate from Greg Renker of Guthy-Renker, a TV marketer of exercise products and videos, who calls ab machines the "hula hoop of the nineties," as quoted in Joe Ueschel, "America's Fascination with the Washboard Look," *USA Today*, 20 May 1996 (27).

Calorie Control Council (28).

Second Harvest (29).

Page 128: *Women's Wear Daily*.

Page 131: Black leather Venus fashions by Debora Iyall.

Pages 133–147: Remaining paper doll fashions by Marilyn Wann.

Page 137: Dashiki fashions by Debora Iyall.

Page 145: Luau fashions by Debora Iyall.

Page 149: Weights of mid-1800s fashions come from Barbara Ehrenreich and Deirdre English, *For Her Own Good: 150 Years of the Experts' Advice to Women* (New York: Anchor, 1978).

Page 154: Housing discrimination findings come from *The Journal of Social Psychology*, 1977.

Page 155: The one in 40,000 figure comes from the TV special *Life in the Fat Lane*. This fun fat fact was researched by Sondra Solovay.

Page 157: Art by Yuri Vann.

Page 158: Upper arm photos by Carol Squires.

Page 160: Muumuu art by Heather Urban.

Page 168: Comparative marriage rates come from Steven L. Gortmaker, et al., "Social and Economic Consequences of Overweight in Adolescence and Young Adulthood," *New England Journal of Medicine* 329, no. 14 (September 1993): 1008–1012.

Page 172: Model, Antonio Cruz; "Tony with Spare Tires" photo, Marilyn Wann.

Page 173: Dial-A-Clue art by Heather Urban.

Page 175: Rubber stamp art by Jack Keely. Alice in Rubberland, P. O. Box 20833, Seattle, Washington 98102.

Page 176: Junior Birdman diagram by Heather Urban.

Page 178: Survey on women who avoid sex comes from *Family Circle* magazine. This fun fat fact was researched by Sondra Solovay.

Page 182: Model, Cath Thompson. Photo, Marilyn Wann.

Page 185: Rubber stamp art by Jack Keely. Alice in Rubberland, P. O. Box 20833, Seattle, Washington 98102.

Page 186: Fig Newton calorie content comes from Fig Newton packaging information.

Page 189: Ganesha art by Heather Urban. All other original trading card art by Jeff Beeson.

PROMOTE A FAT PERSON.

INDEX

WHEN A FAT EMPLOYEE DOES A GOOD JOB, MAKE SURE THEIR MANAGER KNOWS IT.

The author

Marilyn Wann grew up on a cul-de-sac, within earshot of the Disneyland fireworks that celebrate Tinkerbell's nightly descent from the summit of the Matterhorn. She was educated at Sunny Hills High School and Stanford University, where she received B.A. and M.A. degrees in literary theory. Since 1989, she has lived in San Francisco's Western Addition, working as a journalist and zine editor. She also performs with the Padded Lilies, a fat ladies' water ballet troupe. She invites you to visit Hank's Gab Cafe at www.fatso.com.

(Half of the author's proceeds from this book will be donated to the Kids Project of the National Association to Advance Fat Acceptance.)

PHOTO BY ELSA L. T. LEE